Beer Lover's Virginia

Tanya Birch

Globe
Pequot

Guilford, Connecticut

This book is dedicated to my husband, Jim, who's inspired me to develop an even greater appreciation and passion for all things beer.

Globe Pequot

An imprint of Rowman & Littlefield
Distributed by NATIONAL BOOK NETWORK
Copyright © 2016 by Rowman & Littlefield

All photography by the author except for the following:
Blue Mountain Brewery photo of customers in beer garden, courtesy of Mandi Hicks; Hopkins Ale Works photos, courtesy of Sherri Fickel; Starr Hill Brewery, Beer Lover's Pick photo, courtesy of Jack Goodall, marketing manager at Starr Hill; Wild Wolf Brewery photo of customers in outdoor beer garden, courtesy of Mary Wolf; Flying Mouse Beer Lover's Pick photo, courtesy of Frank Moeller; MacDowell Brew Kitchen photo, courtesy of Nils Schnibbe

Maps: Alena Joy Pearce © Rowman & Littlefield

British Library Cataloguing in Publication Information Is Available

Library of Congress Cataloging-in-Publication Data

Birch, Tanya.
  Beer lover's Virginia : best breweries, brewpubs & beer bars / Tanya Birch.
    pages cm
  Includes index.
  ISBN 978-1-4930-1277-0 (paperback : alkaline paper) — ISBN 978-1-4930-2250-2 (e-book) 1. Beer—Virginia—Guidebooks. 2. Breweries—Virginia—Guidebooks. 3. Microbreweries—Virginia—Guidebooks. 4. Bars (Drinking establishments)—Virginia—Guidebooks. I. Title.
  TP577.B525 2016
  338.4'76634209755—dc23
                                                    2015029327

♾™ The paper used in this publication meets the minimum requirements of American National Standard for Information Sciences—Permanence of Paper for Printed Library Materials, ANSI/NISO Z39.48-1992.

All the information in this guidebook is subject to change. We recommend that you call ahead to obtain current information before traveling.

Contents

About the Author

A freelance writer specializing in beer and travel stories, Tanya Birch began her venture into beer-focused writing when she lived in London, England, for 2 years from 2012 until early 2014. While a resident of the United Kingdom, she created a successful blog that featured her beer travel experiences throughout the 20-plus countries she visited abroad. This is her second published book.

Her first published book, entitled *Discovering Vintage Philadelphia*, is a travel guide focused on sharing the stories of timeless bars, delis, restaurants, and shops throughout Philadelphia, Pennsylvania.

Having recently relocated from New Jersey to North Carolina, Tanya looks forward to becoming an expert on the craft beer scene throughout the South, as well as continuing her travel and beer writing projects as she explores new regions of the United States.

She lives in Asheville, North Carolina, with her husband, Jim, and her dog, Barley.

Acknowledgments

Without the support of my husband, Jim, I never would have been able to undertake this project. It was a wonderful adventure, but unfortunately one that I had to carry out alone while Jim managed the everyday responsibilities at home and at his job in New York City.

This project involved lots of time away from home to travel across the entire state of Virginia in a short time period, and when I was home there were many days when I was knee deep in writing. Thank you, Jim, for your 100% support in every way. My love of craft beer has grown from the time I met you back in 2007, from being the assistant brewer in your homebrew operation to being your partner in the many journeys we took together to explore beer throughout our travels abroad. Without these opportunities, I wouldn't have been able to write a book like this.

Thank you to my sister-in-law Liz, my brother-in-law James, and my nieces Claire and Rose for offering me the ideal place to stay—their home—while I visited the breweries throughout the Northern Virginia region. It was wonderful to have a home to go back to every night and to spend time with you all.

Special thanks go to my entire family for their unwavering support throughout my multiple career paths and job transitions over the course of the last few years. Those jobs have spanned investment management, trust administration, human resources consulting, waitressing, and more, and through all of those, you've backed my decisions and have offered your support. I can't express just how important that has been in allowing me to follow my dream of writing.

I've been fortunate to be able to work with a great editor, Tracee Williams, on both this project and my first published book, and this relationship means so much to me. I hope we can continue this great working relationship for years to come.

Though there was a very small percentage of beer establishments I didn't manage to get to due to reasons varying from logistical coordination to an inability to connect with the brewers, I visited approximately 95% of the beer establishments I wrote about in person. I often spoke directly to the owners, head brewers, and people closest to the businesses I wrote about to get my facts for this book. Thank you especially to all those people along the way who took time out of their day to talk to me, to give me a private tour of their breweries, and to share the story of their businesses. It was an amazing journey and I appreciate every moment of it.

The Virginia beer community has many experts who take an active role in the scene, whether they are other beer writers, media experts, members of the Virginia Craft Brewers Guild, or distributors. Everyone I've reached out to in this community has offered to lend a hand. This kind of openness and support was greatly appreciated. It also is representative of the people behind the breweries and the overall current beer culture in Virginia.

Finally, thanks to all those who are reading this right now—to all those other beer enthusiasts out there like me, who seek out the new and exciting beer spots, and who do their part in supporting the craft beer industry as a whole.

Introduction

I have to confess something to you, to all the readers of this book, many who may be Virginia residents; I'm not a resident of Virginia, nor have I ever been a resident of this state. My hope is that this will come as a relief to the majority of readers, because I came into this project with a completely open mind.

No biases, no favoritism. No preconceived notions about which region of Virginia is better than the other, no expectations about who has the best beer or the worst beer.

My primary objective was to understand and write about the state's thriving beer scene at a point in time. To do that, I spent a great deal of time in Virginia throughout the 4 months that I was tasked with writing this book, and this was a wonderful adventure: both traveling around the state and finding out just how diverse it is in its topography, culture, people, and beer.

I visited approximately 95% of the places I wrote about in person, often speaking to the owners, head brewers, and people closest to the business. The only unfortunate part was that I spent most of the time driving around the state by myself, averaging four to six brewery visits per day and driving hours upon hours on the road.

Sadly, this intense travel schedule meant that I usually couldn't partake in pints of beer, but rather, small 1- to 2-ounce samples at each place. The fortunate part was that I was able to benefit from all the to-go beer options, and I now have a coveted collection of Virginia craft beer, including a Virginia growler display.

I have a passion for craft beer and for inspiring others to embrace the world of craft beer. It's a serious passion that began around 2001 when I became a server at a microbrewery while attending college at the University of Pittsburgh. It grew and progressed to a whole new level when I met the love of my life (and now my husband), Jim, 6 years later, who began homebrewing in a 350-square-foot Manhattan studio apartment. Together we explored beer bars and breweries in the New York City area, and undoubtedly spent a little too much of our hard-earned money on learning about them and choosing our favorites (microbrewed beers averaged $6 to $7 per beer then, but today that price could range from $8 to $12).

Our next craft beer discovery journey started while living in London, England, for 2 years. I joined the British CAMRA (Campaign for Real Ale) organization and volunteered at a London beer festival. We traveled to over 20 countries and explored breweries and the craft beer marketplace in each one. I wrote about our experiences on a blog I created—pagirlgoesabroad.com—that proved to be successful, giving me numerous opportunities to meet with some respected brewers across Europe.

Upon moving back home to the US in 2014, I had a lot to catch up on in the American craft beer market. Breweries were and still are opening up at a lightning pace around the US, changing the landscape of the beer industry.

It's almost like a gale force of new breweries and craft beer, and Virginia is clearly part of the storm, a very exciting state to watch out for both now and in the future. State senate bills like SB 604 passed in 2012—enables breweries to sell beer for on-premise consumption—and SB 430—the farm brewery law enacted in 2014—have helped to energize the landscape. Many of the owners and brewers who took a risk to open up their businesses throughout these changing times helped to influence and lobby for the law changes, which now have helped countless other brewers and owners start successful businesses of their own.

In the short time frame between when I send off this book to the time it hits the shelves, many more breweries will have had their grand opening parties. More importantly, they'll be making beer that will showcase all that Virginia has to offer.

Unique beer. Local beer. Beer that will represent their state and their hometowns, generate excitement and pride among residents, and create a sense of community.

I saw that community firsthand throughout my beer travels. I met a myriad of passionate brewers and owners who all have one big mission in mind: creating something that makes people happy.

Having the opportunity to write about all these businesses makes me happy.

How to Use This Guide

This book's purpose is to serve as an informative, sweeping guide to Virginia's current beer scene. Whether or not your level of Virginia craft beer knowledge classifies you as a novice or a pro, this book can be beneficial, a reference guide that you can browse through as needed and carry with you on your beer travels. At the very least it will give you the perfect excuse to plan your next beer-themed vacation.

This book will hopefully trigger your excitement about all the great beer businesses throughout the state, making you aware of Virginia's influence and increasing role within the thriving US craft beer marketplace.

In an effort to help you on your upcoming beer journeys, the beer establishments are first organized according to the general region, then by category of brewery, brewpub, or beer bar, which are further broken down in alphabetical order.

There's one exception to this grouping—Virginia's capital city of Richmond. Though Richmond is technically part of the Central Virginia region, there are more than enough breweries, brewpubs, and beer bars within the city's borders to afford it its own separate section. Understanding that, if you're in Richmond for a visit and are able to enjoy some scenic drives and day trips outside of the city's borders, you should also read through the Central Virginia chapter, which includes some other must-see beer spots, many close to Richmond.

Multilocation brewpubs and beer bars throughout the state's various regions are included in a separate section of the book. Within that section, I share some useful information (history, atmosphere, and what to expect) about each establishment and provide you with addresses for all of their locations within Virginia. Think twice before you think of them as "chain" brewpubs or beer bars. In certain cases, though they're part of a bigger corporation, they're still helping to increase people's exposure to craft beer within their town or region, and each location may be doing something unique; individual brewmasters at the multilocation brewpubs often have some freedom to make alterations and create new recipes. Beer bars have the ability to get one-off kegs to support their local or regional community and small beer businesses.

Differentiating between breweries and brewpubs is not as clear as it once was, but mostly, brewpubs have full restaurants attached and they primarily sell their beer at their brewpub, without participating in much, if any, distribution offsite.

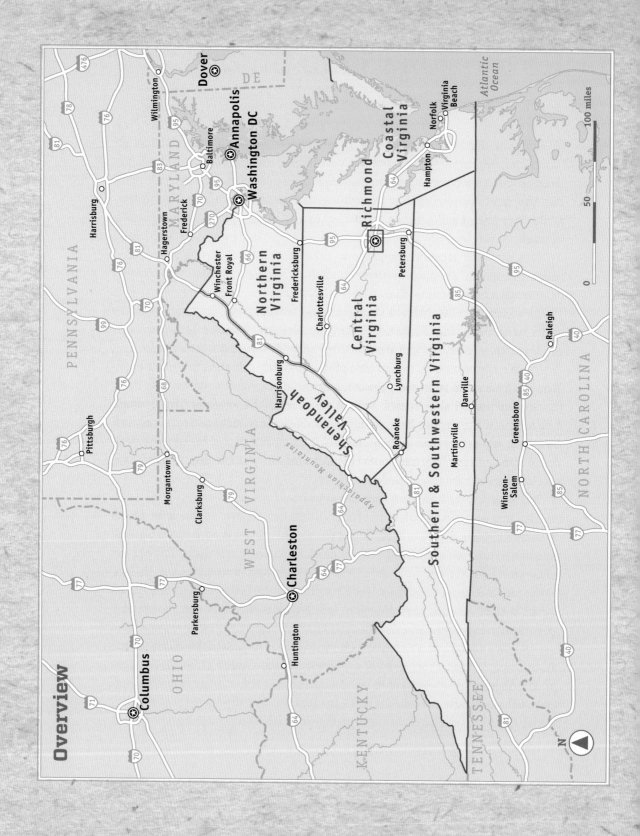

Overview

Breweries, on the other hand, don't always serve food, but usually have tasting rooms where you can sample their beer and perhaps purchase a snack; they also generally distribute offsite and are set up more like a production facility in order to run a larger distribution operation.

Almost all of the brewery write-ups in this book include a Beer Lover's Pick. This could be a beer that the brewery is well known for, one that has won them multiple rave reviews in beer competitions and on beer rating sites. It could be their flagship beer, or one that's available year-round within a wider distribution area. It could be one that meets every criteria of its style category, or one that breaks every criteria of its style category on purpose. Point is, each Beer Lover's Pick is showcased for a reason that will be made obvious within the write-up. Reviewing each Beer Lover's Pick may help you decide which breweries' beers you most prefer, and thereby evaluate which establishments you may want to visit first.

You should understand that, though this guide seeks to be comprehensive, it *does not* claim to cover 100% of the breweries, brewpubs, and craft beer bars in the state. There are undoubtedly a few that will be missed for a number of reasons (e.g., my logistical constraints and deadlines, an inability to establish communication with brewers/owners, overlapping time periods between new breweries' grand openings and book submission and publishing date).

In this book, I also focused more of my time on the breweries and brewpubs rather than the craft beer bars. Countless establishments could be defined as craft beer bars, and rather than highlighting all of them, I've elected to feature a small list of standout craft beer bars, ones that focus primarily on the beer first and have developed a reputation for it, as well as ones that focus on carrying a good and varied selection of beer from local Virginia breweries.

For those who aren't Virginia residents and are just getting acquainted with the state, you should know that it's a vast state and each region offers something unique, in both the beer establishments within that region and the landscapes and environment you can expect to encounter there. Gorgeous mountain towns. Historic town centers. Suburban city life. Coastal beach towns. All of these represent Virginia.

On a map, certain breweries may appear to be in close proximity, and it may look like an easy drive between spots. In reality, it's often a different story, due to a number of reasons, such as heavy traffic in Northern Virginia and the surrounding Washington, DC, metropolitan area, and winding country mountain roads throughout the Shenandoah Valley and Blue Ridge Mountains. These are two examples, but that's not all of them. I learned this the hard way.

There's another alternative if you don't want to worry about the dynamics of driving. You can walk to some beer spots via your own self-guided pub crawl, and you have the option to do that in towns like Charlottesville, Harrisonburg, Richmond, and Staunton. This book includes sample pub crawl itineraries and simple-to-follow maps to show you which way to walk.

In addition to the short guides for all of the breweries, brewpubs, and beer bars, you will also find chapters on:

Beer Festivals: Some exciting beer festivals take place in Virginia. The festivals listed herein are ones that take place every year, almost always during the months they are listed under. This section should help you in planning out your must-visit beer events for the year. Keep your ears and eyes open for others too, as new beer festivals are being planned all the time, and many breweries host their own events or beer festivals too, often advertised on their social media pages and websites.

Beer Bus Tours & Self-Guided Trails: Virginia's various tourism organizations, including the state tourism site—virginia.org—as well as other city and county sites, already offer some great information about brewery happenings. These include self-guided brew trails in certain regions and a variety of companies that offer bus tours centered on scoping out the craft beer spots in Virginia. This section highlights some of those tours and provides you the website addresses where you can find out more detailed information.

BYOB: Brew Your Own Beer: Many professional brewers got their start homebrewing on a much smaller scale. In this book's Brew Your Own Beer section, you will find a select list of homebrew shops in the area. In most cases, these shops have everything you need to brew as well as friendly staff that can help you along, whether you are a beginner looking to start with extract or a seasoned all-grain homebrewer. Following the listing of shops, you will find a selection of a few different clone beer recipes that will give you the opportunity to clone some Virginia beer from great Virginia breweries.

In the Kitchen: Beer pairs well with a number of foods, and it can also be used to enhance dishes as well. The In the Kitchen section features recipes from breweries and brewpubs that incorporate their beer. You might be surprised at how versatile a cooking ingredient it is when used in everything from appetizers to entrees, dressings to desserts. Use the recommended beer when you can, but feel free to substitute a beer in the same style if the listed beer is not available.

Glossary of Terms

ABV: Alcohol by volume—the percentage of alcohol in a beer. A typical mass-market domestic beer is a little less than 5% ABV.

Ale: Beer brewed with top-fermenting yeast. Ales are quicker to brew than lagers, which can require weeks of aging at cold temperatures. Popular styles of ales include pale ales, amber ales, stouts, and porters.

Altbier: A German style of ale, typically brown in color, smooth, and malty.

Barleywine: Not a wine at all but a high-ABV ale that originated in England. English versions tend to have a sweeter, maltier balance while American versions often have large amounts of hops.

Barrel of beer: Production of beer is measured in barrels. A barrel equals 31 gallons.

Beer: An alcoholic beverage brewed with malt, water, hops, and yeast.

Beer bar: A bar that focuses on carrying craft or fine imported beers.

Bitter: An English bitter is an English-style ale, more hoppy than an English mild. Brewed for drinkability typically with a slightly lower alcohol content than normal.

Bock: A German-style lager, typically stronger than the typical lager.

Bomber: Most beers are packaged in 12-ounce bottles. Bombers are 22-ounce bottles.

Brewpub: Typically a restaurant, but sometimes a bar, that brews its own beers on premises.

Cask ales: Also known as real ales, cask ales are naturally carbonated and are usually poured with a handpump rather than forced out with carbon dioxide or nitrogen.

Clone beer: A homebrew recipe based on a commercial beer.

Contract brewery: A company that does not have its own brewery and pays someone else to brew and bottle its beer.

Craft beer: High-quality, flavorful beer made by craft brewers (see next definition).

Craft brewer: According to the Brewers Association, a craft brewer is small (annual production of 6 million barrels of beer or less), independent (less than 25 percent of the craft brewery is owned or controlled [or equivalent economic interest] by an alcoholic beverage industry member that is not itself a craft brewer), and traditional (a majority of its total beverage alcohol volume in beers whose flavor derives from traditional or innovative brewing ingredients and their fermentation).

Double: The word double most often refers to a higher-alcohol version of a beer, most typically used in reference to a double, or imperial, IPA. It can also be used as an American translation of a Belgian dubbel, a style of Belgian ale.

ESB: Extra-special bitter. A traditional malt-heavy English pub ale with low bitterness, usually served on cask.

Gastropub: A beer-centric bar or pub that exhibits the same amount of care selecting its foods as it does its beers.

Gose: A style of beer with a sour wheat flavor that originated in Germany. Usually has a grain bill made up of at least 50% malted wheat.

Growler: A half-gallon jug of beer, often glass. Many brewpubs sell growlers of their beers to go.

Hops: Hops are flowers used in beers to produce aroma, bitterness, and flavor. Nearly every beer in the world has hops.

IBU: International bittering units, which are used to measure how bitter a beer is.

Imperial: A higher-alcohol version of a regular-strength beer.

IPA: India pale ale. A popular style of ale created in England that has taken a decidedly American twist over the years. Often bitter, thanks to more hops used than in other styles of beer.

Kölsch: A light, refreshing German-style ale. Style originated in Cologne, Germany.

Lager: Beer brewed with bottom-fermenting yeast. Takes longer and is harder to brew than ales. Popular styles of lagers include black lagers, doppelbocks, pilsners, and Vienna lagers.

Malt: Typically barley malt, but sometimes wheat malt. Malt provides the fermentable sugar in beers. The more fermentable sugar, the higher the ABV in a beer. Without malt, a beer would be too bitter from the hops.

Mash: Brewer's term for the steeping of the hot water and grains that activates the malt enzymes and converts the starches from the grains into fermentable sugars.

Microbrewery: A brewery that brews fewer than 15,000 barrels of beer a year.

Nanobrewery: A brewery that brews 4 barrels of beer per batch or less.

Pilsner: A style of German or Czech lager, usually light in color.

Porter: A dark ale, similar to the stout but with fewer roasted characters.

Pounders: 16-ounce cans.

Quad: A strong Belgian-style ale, typically sweet and high in alcohol.

Regional brewery: A brewery that brews up to 6 million barrels of beer a year.

Russian imperial stout: A stout is a dark, heavy beer. A Russian imperial stout is a higher-alcohol, thicker-bodied version of a regular stout.

Saison: Also known as a Belgian or French farmhouse ale. It can be fruity, and it can also be peppery. Usually refreshing.

Seasonal: A beer that is brewed only at a certain time of year to coincide with the seasons.

Session beer: A low-alcohol beer, one you can have several of in one long drinking "session."

Stout: A dark beer brewed with roasted malts.

Strong ale: A style of ale that is typically both hoppy and malty and can be aged for years.

Tap takeover: An event where a bar or pub hosts a brewery and has several of its beers on tap.

Triple (Tripel): A Belgian-style ale, typically lighter in color than a dubbel but higher in alcohol.

Wheat beer: Beers such as hefeweizens and witbiers, that are brewed using wheat malt along with barley malt.

Wort: The sweet liquid that is extracted from the mixing of hot water and malt (mash). Wort contains all the sugars that will be fermented by the yeast to produce alcohol.

Yeast: The living organism in beer that causes the sugars to ferment and become alcohol.

Northern Virginia

It's no surprise that Northern Virginia is a prime spot to live due to its close proximity to Washington, DC, and equally no surprise that major companies in the energy, technology, finance, and communications fields have decided to establish their corporate headquarters here.

What does come as a surprise is that there were practically no craft production breweries in the DC vicinity from the end of Prohibition in 1933 until just a few short years ago, when Port City Brewing set up home in Alexandria. Since then, breweries have sprouted up fast and frequently, and this region is now home to more than thirty craft beer–focused businesses, with more opening at a fast clip.

You might associate this region with its heavily populated suburban towns and its large sprawls of shopping plazas and office complexes. You should also associate this region with its incredible history and historic battlefields, its farms and wineries, and its large parks and wonderful outdoor recreational trails—like the 45-mile Washington and Old Dominion Trail that stretches from Arlington to Purcellville.

Breweries are now part of this vibrant area everywhere you look, whether that is inside one of the many office complexes or shopping plazas, or at an ideal resting spot after a long cycle ride across the vast rail trail.

Breweries

ADROIT THEORY BREWING COMPANY

404 Browning Ct., Unit C, Purcellville, VA 20132; (703) 722-3144; adroit-theory.com;
@AdroitTheory
Founded: 2014 **Founders:** Mark and Nina Osborne **Brewer:** Greg Skotzko **Flagship
Beer:** N/A **Year-Round Beers:** N/A **Seasonals/Special Releases:** All beers are small
batch, special release beers **Tours:** No **Taproom:** Thurs, 4 to 8 p.m.; Fri and Sat, 12 to 8
p.m.; Sun, 12 to 6 p.m.

Nontraditional in every sense of the word, the team at Adroit Theory defines
their beers as *esoteric*. You won't find session beers. You should not expect the
brewers to serve you beers that follow *Reinheitsgebot* either (the Bavarian purity law
of 1516 that defines three basic ingredients to be used in the production of beer—
water, barley, and hops).

The brewery and tasting room opened in early 2014. For the first 6 months head
brewer Greg Skotzko said it was "like a speakeasy," because there were no visible

Beer Lover's Pick

B/A/Y/S (Black As Your Soul) Imperial Stout
Style: Russian Imperial Stout
ABV: 9.1%
Availability: Rotating on tap and in 350ml bottles

Aged in a brandy barrel, the color
of this beer is very dark black, fit-
tingly matching its name. Heavily
hopped at 80 IBU, it has roasty,
caramel aromas and a smoked,
earthy flavor. The beer was aged
on reclaimed American chestnut
wood, which results in a flavor
that's different from the typical
imperial stout.

signs. You had to be in the know to drive around to the back of the industrial complex, then pick the correct plain gray door among other similar gray doors in the complex to get to the tasting room.

Today there are visible Adroit Theory signs, but you will still feel like you've discovered a hidden treasure once you walk inside to enormously tall ceilings, a spacious tasting room, and a large bar area with space for 24 taps. Sample beer from one of the stools at the bar or when you sit with your friends at a cocktail table made from a barrel. Beer is available for takeout through growlers and through limited release offerings of 350ml bottles (all of which are bottled by hand). One wall displays their souvenirs and beer memorabilia for sale, while toward the back of the public tasting space you can look through glass windows and check out the small pilot system where they brew most of their beers, resulting in about 1-barrel batches. When they find something they love, they'll often contract to work with another brewery nearby to use its production facility, where they're able to brew larger 30- to 60-barrel batches.

Though they don't define themselves as having one focus or regular style of beer, they do tend to produce high-alcohol beers (generally over 7.5% ABV) with an emphasis on barrel aging. You will see some of those actual barrels aging throughout the tasting room. Past beers have included a saison inspired by absinthe called the **T/B/D (The Perfect Drug)**, its name in honor of a Nine Inch Nails song, as well as an **Experimental—Belgian Tripel with Fruit Loops (Ghost 088)**, evoking the smells of red, green, and orange Froot Loops. During my visit they were making **Key Lime Pie Stout**. To make this beer, graham crackers were used in the mash tun.

The names and ingredients in their beers are paired with unique artwork and themes, which are often described in more detail on their website. Greg says the whole team works together "making sure the product matches the creativeness of the branding."

ADVENTURE BREWING CO. *First Brewery when we moved to VA*
33 Perchwood Dr., Stafford, VA 22405; (540) 242-8876; adventurebrewing.com; @AdventureBrewCo
Founded: 2014 **Founders:** Tim Bornholtz, John Viarella, Stan Johnson **Brewers:** Bryan Link, Tim Bornholtz, John Viarella, Stan Johnson **Flagship Beer:** Expedition IPA **Year-Round Beers:** Expedition IPA, Backpack Wheat, Stiletto Stout, Super Power Pale Ale **Seasonals/Special Releases:** Second Ascent Double IPA, Bobsled Winter Ale, Go East Young Man, Bookworm Brown, Wicked Nymph (see website for most updated list) **Tours:** Upon request **Taproom:** Wed through Fri, 3:30 to 10 p.m.; Sat, 12 to 10 p.m.; Sun, 12 to 6 p.m.

Many brewery owners discover their love for the brewery industry through their beginnings as homebrewers, but only a small percentage of homebrewers make the effort to turn their hobby into a business, especially those who are still working full-time jobs, as is the case for Adventure Brewing owners Tim, John, and Stan. All three began homebrewing in the late '90s, followed by brief intervals of time where the homebrewing was less frequent due to their work lives, daily work commutes to and from Washington, DC, and efforts to maximize family time. Eventually all three guys came together and brewed more regularly for fun. Their beer was a hit at frequent neighborhood gatherings. Soon after they realized it was time to turn their beer-making operation at home into a business, and they have been officially open since the spring of 2014.

The owners confirm that the best part of their day-to-day lives in the brewery is "seeing the faces of people we don't know drinking our beer and enjoying it." All three live in Stafford County and are proud of their community, so proud that one of the Stafford County landmarks, a tree that was once next to the Stafford County Courthouse building, has been repurposed into their tasting room bar top.

Adventure Brewing's warehouse location in Stafford is an ideal gathering spot for town residents who want to chat over a beer or attend one of the brewery's many events. Wednesday is a designated game night and Thursday is trivia night. Friday nights often showcase live music like jazz, blues, or bluegrass between 8 and 10 p.m., while Saturday night is movie night, when a projector is set up in a section adjacent to the bar. Food trucks set up outside on busy tasting room days.

Beer Lover's Pick

Expedition IPA
Style: India Pale Ale
ABV: 5.9%
Availability: Year-round on tap

White wine and citrus flavors make this beer a less traditional, aromatic India pale ale. In today's craft beer world where hoppiness is often taken to an extreme level, Adventure's Expedition IPA reaffirms why extreme isn't always better. It's balanced while still maintaining its hoppy attributes.

They strive to make their beers full flavored and balanced—accessible beers for their community—as is the case with their **Backpack Wheat**, a traditional German wheat beer recipe with a smooth finish. In the cold months, warm up with their **Stiletto Stout**. At 7% ABV it has a nice maltiness and hints of chocolate and coffee. For a twist from the traditional styles, they have experimented with some nontraditional ingredients, like their **Go East Young Man** wheat beer, a tribute for Elvis's birthday, made with peanut butter, banana, and marshmallow fluff. Be sure to ask about just how messy it was trying to add marshmallow to the brew tanks.

BADWOLF BREWING COMPANY
9776 Center St., Manassas, VA 20110; (571) 208-1064; badwolfbrewingcompany.com; @BadWolfBrewingC
Founded: 2012 **Founders:** Jeremy and Sarah Meyers **Brewers:** Jeremy Meyers, Jesse Johnson, Ryan McLeod, Bryan Bell, Claire Ainsworth **Flagship Beer:** N/A **Year-Round Beers:** N/A **Seasonals/Special Releases:** All beers are small batch and rotating **Tours:** No **Taproom:** Wed and Thurs, 4 to 9 p.m.; Fri, 3 to 10 p.m.; Sat, 2 to 10 p.m.; Sun, 1 to 6 p.m.

If you've never homebrewed yourself but have always wanted to try it, you should consider a visit to BadWolf Brewing Company, tucked into a shopping plaza not far from Old Town Manassas. You can see all the action and hard work involved in brewing firsthand as you sip on a tasting tray of the draft beer choices available that day. The beers constantly change due to both the staff's experimentation with different styles and the fact that they're using a 1-barrel brew system, stationed on the back counter directly behind the bar. During my visit one of the brewers was stirring the brew kettle with one hand and filling up a growler with another hand. That's multitasking at its finest.

By the time you read this, BadWolf will have opened a second location with a 10-barrel electric system, and much more space—at least six times the space as their new location is over 6,000 feet—than the one they're currently producing beer from. That will allow them to begin bottling their beers too.

In the meantime, when you visit their small, intimate location at Center Street, you'll get the full locals experience and have the opportunity to talk to the customers sitting at a table or at one of the six barstools near you. Much of the interior, like the tables, shelving, and even the bar, was built or carried in by the owners, brewers, and friends of the brewers.

When asked about day-to-day life at BadWolf Brewing, assistant brewer Claire Ainsworth said, "Every day's completely different. We like to joke that we're consistently inconsistent."

At BadWolf, just as every day is different, every beer is different—on purpose. They are consistently experimenting with all kinds of combinations. They're willing to try both perfecting standard styles like the **Cascade Pale Ale**, a crisp, balanced American pale ale brewed with Cascade hops, as well as the off the wall styles, like a **Peanut Butter and Jelly Stout**. One of their recent popular beers was an oak-aged imperial IPA at 8.6% ABV, named **You Will Not Like This IPA**. Turned out that customers did like it after all.

Beer Lover's Pick

Sorachi SMASH
Style: Specialty Beer, Spiced Belgian-Style
ABV: 7.5%
Availability: Rotating on tap
Sorachi is named for the Sorachi Ace hop that has a bold, unique flavor. Its lemony, herbal essence alone makes for a great-tasting beer. Pair that hop with the right malt (and the right other base ingredients like the best type of yeast strain) and you have a full-flavored enjoyable drink.

BELLY LOVE BREWING COMPANY

725 E. Main St., Purcellville, VA 20132; (540) 441-3159; bellylovebrewing.com; @BellyLoveBeer

Founded: 2014 **Founders:** Tolga and Kathleen Baki **Brewer:** Tolga Baki **Flagship Beer:** Shut the Fook Up **Year-Round Beers:** Shut the Fook Up, My Bitter X, Eye of Jupiter, Narcissist **Seasonals/Special Releases:** Brown Willie, Bunk Off!, Auld Resolutions, Boom Choco LoCo Boom (usually two rotating seasonals) **Tours:** No **Taproom:** Mon, 3 to 10 p.m.; Thurs and Fri, 3 to 10 p.m.; Sat, 12 to 10 p.m.; Sun, 12 to 8 p.m.

Within one shopping plaza in Purcellville, you can accomplish all of your errands for the day—fill up your car with gasoline, swing by the pharmacy, and setttle your accounts at the bank—and also enjoy a warm, peaceful afternoon or evening out at a brewery. You'll never think the same way about shopping complexes again once you try some delicious food and drinks at Belly Love Brewing.

There are mouthwatering small plates that change seasonally. Plates such as pork belly tacos, shrimp tempura, and artichoke beignets with lemon herb aioli brilliantly couple with inventively named beers such as **Shut the Fook Up**, a balanced pale ale with nice malt flavors and well-known, popular hop varieties such as East Kent Goldings and German Hallertau. Or try the **My Bitter X**, just as bitter as a bitter ex-relationship might be, with hops such as Centennial, Columbus, and Citra, but

also balanced with some great floral notes. To spice it up even more, there's often a nice seasonal beer on tap, such as **Auld Resolutions**, a brown ale brewed with ginger, orange peel, and cinnamon.

Beer Lover's Pick

Eye of Jupiter
Style: Oatmeal Stout
ABV: 6.2%
Availability: Year-round on tap
This oatmeal stout is a grown-up milk shake layered with coffee and chocolate overtones. Perfect for a cold day, but really any temperature will do; beers with this kind of malt complexity should be enjoyed whether it's cold, warm, or hot.

Other Nanobreweries to Check Out in Northern VA

BEER HOUND BREWING
201 Waters Place, #102, Culpeper, VA 22701; beerhoundbrewery.com
Located in the arts district in downtown Culpeper, this brewery was founded by Kenny Thacker who opened the brewery in 2012. By October 2014, with the help of beer friends and entrepreneurs Frank Becker and Rick Cash, they opened doors at a new establishment in Culpeper. Beer names are creative, all named after famous hounds, including the Teufelhunde Belgian Ale, Apollo Hefeweizen, and Teddy American Cream Ale.

Sample all of the above selections while you sit in zen-like surroundings at the couch in front or at one of the many tables surrounding the L-shaped bar. Alternatively, stand up by the bar to enjoy conversation with other customers or with the insightful, relaxed, and happy staff. There are no barstools and no TVs by design. Brick walls, fun industrial lighting, and, as co-owner Kathleen Baki suggests, "denim blue jean"–colored walls, complete the look that pays tribute to the Belly Love Brewing name.

As you walk to the bathrooms at the back of the taproom, you'll get a direct view of the 7-barrel brew system where you'll often find co-owner Tolga Baki putting in some tough physical labor (it's a very manual system) in order to keep the beer flowing. His dad is often also in the brewhouse area helping out.

BLUE AND GRAY BREWING COMPANY
3300 Dill Smith Dr., Fredericksburg, VA 22408; (540) 538-2379; blueandgraybrewingco.com
Founded: 2002 **Founder:** Jeffrey Fitzpatrick **Brewer:** Patrick Byrne **Flagship Beer:** Fred Red Irish Ale **Year-Round Beers:** Fred Red Irish Ale, Blue and Gray Classic Lager, Falmouth American Pale Ale, Stonewall Stout **Seasonals/Special Releases:** Temporary Insanity Imperial Stout, Minor Dementia Imperial Stout, Chocolate Raspberry Stout, Virginia Hefeweizen, Oktoberfest Lager, Spiced Winter Ale, Belgian Ale, Washington's Cherry Wheat **Tours:** Sat, 10 a.m. to 2 p.m. (and groups 15 or more by appointment) **Brewpub hours:** Tues through Sat, 11 a.m. to 10 p.m.

The historic town of Fredericksburg, where Blue and Gray Brewing is based, was an important site for some notable battles during the Civil War, hence the name Blue and Gray Brewing, after the uniform colors of the Union and Confederate soldiers.

It began as strictly a manufacturing facility, but in 2010 they moved buildings and subsequently added a brewpub. The brewpub and brewery today is a warehouse from the 1920s transformed into a rustic space where you can enjoy pub food and microbrewed beer. From your seat within the pub, you can see through the windows to get a view of the brew tanks. If you want an official tour, stop by on Saturday when you can get a guided tour of the process and sample the wort directly from the kettle.

If you prefer classic styles, try the **Blue & Gray Classic Lager**, described as a crisp, smooth classic Munich Helles–style lager or the **Falmouth American Pale Ale**, which has all the traits of a signature American pale ale. For those a little more adventurous and craving a bold flavor packed with a strong punch, the seasonal **Temporary Insanity Imperial Stout**, at 10.2% ABV, is a full-bodied Russian imperial stout with deep complex aromas and flavors to match.

Food inconsistent
Fred Red was good
Was very
Bought a
Adventure

The beer is only sold within a 30-mile radius of the Fredericksburg area, so if you're from out of town, you may want to swing by the side entrance after your visit to the brewpub where you can take beer home with you at a separate designated growler filling station.

Beer Lover's Pick

Fred Red Ale
Style: Irish Ale
ABV: 6.8%
Availability: Year-round
Blue and Gray Brewing Co's flagship ale, the Fred Red Ale, is ideal for those who prefer malt over hops. Brewed in the Irish ale style, it's a great choice to drink onsite at the brewpub—an Irish ale paired with the same laid-back relaxed atmosphere you might find at an old historic pub in Ireland's countryside. Its character and deep red color mimic that of the Irish ale, yet the 6.8% ABV is higher than many of the old ales from Ireland that were originally brewed to be session ales.

CORCORAN BREWING COMPANY

205 Hirst Rd., Suite 105, Purcellville, VA 20132; (540) 441-3102; corcoranbrewing
.com; @CorcoranBrew
Founded: 2011 **Founders:** Jim and Lori Corcoran **Brewer:** Kevin Bills **Flagship Beer:**
LoCo **Year-Round Beers:** LoCo, Corky's Irish Red, Slainte Stout, P'Ville **Seasonals/**
Special Releases: Jeb Stuart Stout, Oatlands, Padawan Pumpkin, Waterford Wit **Tours:**
Upon request **Taproom:** Wed and Thurs, 3 to 9 p.m.; Fri and Sat, 12 to 10 p.m.; Sun, 12
to 6 p.m.

Before Corcoran Brewing, there was Corcoran Vineyards, a small family-run winery that opened to the public in 2004 in Loudoun County. In 2011, Jim and
Lori Corcoran decided to branch out to the brewery business, and for a time both the
winery and the brewery were at the same location, until they moved the brewery a
few miles away, establishing its new home within the town of Purcellville.

Today you can travel to Corcoran Vineyards to enjoy their wine and their newest
beverage-making venture—hard cider—and then continue on to Corcoran Brewing
to enjoy the atmosphere of the brewery and tasting room, or vice versa. At the
brewery, expect food trucks and live music on warm, busy days (check out the event

Padawan Pumpkin Ale

Style: Pumpkin Ale

ABV: 6%

Availability: Seasonal (fall)

With Corcoran's use of local pumpkins and honey from nearby farms, this amber-colored ale is the best treat on a fall day, when the humidity of the summer months is finally behind you. Awaken your taste buds with the sensational pumpkin pie spice notes. Though it's a fall beer, you won't mind drinking it into the winter.

calendar on their website). Regular customers might want to consider Corcoran's mug club, where for an annual fee you'll get a customized mug as well as discounts on beer and brewery merchandise.

The family's roots in the winery business are evident in their beer tasting room, a rustic, warm space with wine barrel tables open to the brewery. Front and center is the bar, fitting snugly between the brew space to the right of the entrance and the tasting room tables to the left, where you can expect an average of 12 beers on draft.

Hopheads might prefer the **LoCo**, a medium-bodied West Coast–style IPA, named after their slogan, "Great Beer with a LoCo attitude." For those not from the area, LoCo stands for Loudoun County (the county where Corcoran Brewing is based). Seasonal choices include the **Mosby's Raider**, an imperial IPA, named after John Mosby, whose raiders eluded the Union army in this area during the Civil War. For a refreshing choice during the summer months, try the **Waterford Wit**, a Belgian witbier with notes of coriander and orange peel. When it's cold outside, it'll be warm and cozy inside Corcoran Brewing, where you can bring your kids and even bring your dog. On those days, you can't leave without trying the **Jeb Stuart Stout**, an imperial stout aged in Bowman Distilling Bourbon barrels.

CROOKED RUN BREWING

205 Harrison St. SE, Suite B, Leesburg, VA 20175; (571) 918-4446; crookedrunbrewing.com; @Crookedrunbrew
Founded: 2013 **Founders:** Jake Endres, Lee Rogan **Brewer:** Jake Endres, Lee Rogan **Flagship Beer:** Red Kölsch **Year-Round Beers:** Storm IPA, Shadow of Truth, **Seasonals/Special Releases:** Stovepipe Smoked Pumpkin Porter, You're Cool Cucumber Mint Wheat **Tours:** Upon request **Taproom:** Wed and Thurs, 4 to 10 p.m.; Fri, 4 p.m. to 12 a.m.; Sat, 1 p.m. to 12 a.m.; Sun, 1 to 6 p.m.

It's a gutsy move to start your own business at any age, let alone immediately after you graduate from college. That's what Jake Endres did when he realized employment prospects were low and that he wanted to take the 6 years of homebrewing skills he had acquired to a brand new level. He put together the business plans for Crooked Run Brewing and funded a project on Kickstarter, which helped him to raise the money he needed to set up in downtown Leesburg. When he opened Crooked

Run, he was in his mid-20s; Jake proudly shares that he and co-owner Lee Rogan are the youngest brewery owners in the state of Virginia today.

They found a small, charming spot for their nanobrewery operation in Leesburg's historic Market Station, a restored freight station now used for commerce, and a convenient place before or after partaking in other entertainment options in downtown, from restaurants to independent shops to a beach-themed bar, MacDowell Brew Kitchen (see Beer Bars within this chapter), where you can also go for a great selection of other craft beer.

Enter to find the 1.5-barrel electric system squeezed in along a narrow walkway to your right. The tasting room includes a few tables and a small bar, large enough to showcase their regular rotating beer varieties, where the Crooked Run team offers a variety of styles using local ingredients. Expect to see an average of 5 beers on tap during your visit.

Crooked Run Brewing's motto is "seek truth, cherish nature" and consequently the beer names often reflect truth and nature themes. Try the **Storm**, an American IPA intensified with Galaxy hops, or for a bigger massive hop flavor try the **Force of Nature**, a double IPA using Zythos hops. The **Realize Truth**, an elderberry quadrupel made with candied syrup and elderberry juice from a local winery, is bright and Belgiany. For a smoother, lighter in alcohol beer, the **Red Kölsch**, their flagship beer, is an Irish and German kölsch at 4.5% ABV.

Beer Lover's Pick

Shadow of Truth
Style: Belgian Dark Ale
ABV: 9%
Availability: Rotating
This beer is dark black in color with a very smooth finish. Its complexity is evident in its dark roasted malts, followed by that signature Belgian tripel fruity sweetness. The sweetness creates the right amount of subtlety, fortunately not overpowering in its sweetness profile as you might imagine for a 9% ABV beer.

FAIR WINDS BREWING COMPANY

7000 Newington Rd., Suites K&L, Lorton, VA 22079; (703) 372-2001;
fairwindsbrewing.com; @FairWindsBrew
Founded: 2014 **Founders:** Casey Jones, Charlie Buettner **Brewers:** Charlie Buettner,
Will Cook **Flagship Beers:** Howling Gale IPA, Quayside Kölsch **Year-Round Beers:**
Running Light Red, Following Cs Pale Ale, Howling Gale IPA, Quayside Kölsch **Seasonals/**
Special Releases: Flemish Stout (see website for specifics) **Tours:** Sat at 1, 3 and 5
p.m. (tours are free, sign up early) **Taproom:** Wed and Thurs, 4 to 8 p.m.; Fri, 2 to 10
p.m.; Sat, 12 to 9 p.m.; Sun, 12 to 5 p.m.

While a student in an entrepreneurship class in his senior year at the US Coast Guard Academy, Fair Winds founder Casey Jones wrote his business plan for a square-rigged brewpub. Though only an assignment, his goal to be in the beer business was a serious one, but one that he stresses didn't happen overnight, as it wasn't until 20-some years later, in early 2015, when Fair Winds Brewing officially opened for business. It's never too late to turn your dream into a reality.

During his years in the Coast Guard, he was often homebrewing too. The entire homebrewing process had to be accomplished in short periods of time when he was off patrol, leaving a "tight window to ferment and consume the beer," as Casey described to me. That's why serving the local homebrewing community in Fairfax County is important to the staff at Fair Winds Brewing today, where they hope to serve as a resource for the community and eventually offer some ongoing homebrew contests, with the winner getting the chance to brew on a larger system at the brewery.

Quayside Kölsch
Style: Golden Ale
ABV: 4.5%
Availability: Year-round on tap

Head brewer Charlie Buettner had to learn a thing or two about brewing kölsch beer during his previous brewing job at Mad Fox Brewing Company; Mad Fox's owner and executive brewer Bill Madden is known for his smooth and flavorful German-style kölsch beers. This new Fair Winds kölsch is Charlie's original recipe, his approach to the much-loved beer style that originated in Cologne, Germany. German hops and German malts contribute to this light, crisp beer.

The tasting room is open and spacious, with garage doors that open in the warmer months and ambient lighting; the Fair Winds team hopes this makes it a welcoming environment to be used as a hang-out place, where you can bring your entire family along. A cart against one wall of the tasting room is filled with board games for the kids, or those adults who want to pretend they're kids again.

Along that same wall, you can look through glass windows into the large 30-barrel brewhouse, which will be producing large 930-gallon batches of beer like the **Howling Gale IPA**, a double dry-hopped West Coast–style IPA. Head brewer Charlie Buettner hopes to highlight their hop-forward approach in many of their beer offerings, including in choices like the **Following Cs Pale Ale**, that utilizes a bunch of hops whose names start with a C, like Cascade and Columbus.

Prior to Fair Winds' opening, there wasn't a bigger-scale packaging brewery in Fairfax County (though there is another nanobrewery—Forge Brew Works—located right up the road; see next write-up). Fair Winds Brewing is helping to change that for their community, and their distribution territory currently spans about 45 different places in Northern Virginia.

Northern Virginia

As you leave the brewery's tasting room, you'll see a sign made out of wood that reads "May you always have fair winds and following seas," a saying that sailors often use to wish each other a pleasant experience and journey onward to their next destination. The experience you have at Fair Winds' tasting room is geared to be just as pleasant—and an easy journey onward for many residents of the local community, who can visit a brewery near their home.

FORGE BREW WORKS

8532 Terminal Rd., Suite L, Lorton, VA 22079; (703) 372-2979; forgebrewworks.com; @ForgeBrewWorks
Founded: 2013 **Founders:** Kerri and Matt Rose **Brewer:** Matt Rose **Flagship Beers:** Belgian Blonde **Year-Round Beers:** Farmhouse Ale, Slake IPA, Oatmeal Stout, Roggenbier, Belgian Blonde, Petite Saison, Seaward DIPA **Seasonals/Special Releases:** Elder Gods Ale (see website for more seasonal/special releases) **Tours:** Available by reservation **Taproom:** Wed and Thurs, 4 to 8 p.m.; Fri, 4 to 10 p.m.; Sat, 12 to 10 p.m.; Sun, 12 to 6 p.m.

Hard Work Tastes Better. That's Forge Brew Works' motto, and the one that Matt Rose, co-founder of the brewery along with his wife, Kerri Rose, promotes day in and day out in the brewery. Starting small in 2013 with a 1-barrel system, they upgraded within 6 months to a 5-barrel system. In recent years they produced about

500 barrels annually, and this year they are on track to at least double that amount, with a plan to quadruple it when they purchase new and bigger equipment (planning for the new equipment is in the works, so be sure to look out for announcements in future months).

The brewery is situated at a corner spot among other industrial spaces, a plain brick building from the outside, though easily spotted if their beer truck is parked outside—an old police van, or as it's known to most, a paddy wagon. Painted in black and red with the Forge Brew Works logo, this is a cool beer truck, one that is undoubtedly noticed from afar when it transports beer around the area. A funny coincidence is that their current 5-barrel brew system is rumored to have been produced by prisoners as part of a work outreach system back in the mid '90s.

Don't worry, you're not walking into a prison, but a casual tasting room experience inside, an unadorned space that's the perfect unwind spot after a day of hard work. It's open to all, including children and dogs, and there are often events like trivia nights and live music on weekends.

With an average of 10 to 12 beers on tap, you're guaranteed to have lots of choices of beer, like the **Roggenbier**. Forge's Roggenbier is basically a hefeweizen base but instead of using wheat in their grain bill, they use rye, which makes this a smooth and full-of-flavor beer with a hint of spiciness from the rye. In the fall, look out for the popular **Elder Gods Ale**, a 12% ABV old ale made with raspberries and cocoa nibs. Or try some of their farmhouse and Belgian-inspired beers that you will often see on tap due to Matt's love of Belgian-style beers.

Beer Lover's Pick

Belgian Blonde
Style: Blonde Ale
ABV: 7.2%
Availability: Year-round on tap
The sweetness and banana-like flavors from the Belgian yeast takes this traditional blonde ale beer up a notch. It has a great golden color and a sessionable taste, though beware, as the alcohol content is not as sessionable—it will creep up on you at 7.2% ABV.

HERITAGE BREWING CO.

9436 Center Point Ln., Manassas, VA 20110; (571) 358-8463; heritagebrewing.com; @HeritageBrews

Founded: 2013 **Founders:** Sean and Ryan Arroyo **Brewer:** Bo Elliott **Flagship Beers:** American Expedition Honey Ginger Wheat Ale, Freedom Isn't Free IPA, Kings Mountain Scotch Ale, Revolution American Amber Ale, The Teddy Pale Ale **Year-Round Beers:** Same as Flagships **Seasonals/Special Releases:** Bradford, The Battle of White Marsh, Sovereign Stout, Ironsides **Tours:** Sat, 12 p.m. and 1 p.m. **Taproom:** Thurs and Fri, 5 to 9 p.m.; Sat, 12 to 9 p.m.; Sun, 12 to 6 p.m.

Your eyes are first drawn to the enormous American flag taking over the wall behind the brewing equipment. It has all the usual allure that you'd expect of a brewery: shiny, clean brew tanks in the same open room as the tasting room. There is a long bar, weaving around to conform to the corners of the walls that hide the large refrigeration storage behind it.

Look closer and you'll notice a few other details, all ones that make Heritage Brewing a must-see stop on your beer travels. Above the shiny brew tanks—a 20-barrel brew system—you'll see wires and hoses and pipes exposed and hanging in makeshift ways, obvious indications of the hard work that went into getting this brewery set up. "We installed the system ourselves," owner Sean Arroyo tells me. Sean served in the Marines for many years before he retired and started Heritage, which he co-founded with his brother Ryan, who is still actively serving in the

military. Not only did they install the system, but they also laid the concrete, and they made the bar from pallet wood that they received from a farm and sheet metal they obtained from an old barn in southern Virginia.

Beer Lover's Pick

Oak-Aged Kings Mountain
Style: Oak-Aged Scot-American Ale
ABV: 11%
Availability: Limited release, sold in 750ml bottles

Its deep, dark pour tempts you to taste it, but in truth that only hints at all the goodness that's ahead. It's malty. It's textured, with many different layers, each better than the next, aged in an oak barrel from local Catoctin Creek Distilling Company in nearby Purcellville. 100% American-sourced ingredients and local base malts. 100% deliciousness.

The same hard work is invested into making the beer, which is made with 100% American-sourced ingredients and base malts. Packaging manager Chris Hampel told me he recently squeezed 240 oranges by hand for use in their **Revolution**, an American amber ale brewed with oranges. An Americana theme is evident in their beer names. Beer enthusiasts who prefer maltiness will enjoy the **Kings Mountain Scotch Ale**, "named after a patriot victory in the Revolutionary War fought between Scot-patriots and Scot-loyalists." Or try the lighter-bodied **American Expedition**, a honey ginger wheat ale named for the Lewis and Clark discovery journey.

The beers are all designed to be smooth and well balanced, fit for craft beer fans as well as people who are just starting to discover what's so amazing about craft beer. Expect an average of 8 to 12 beers on draft during your visit. Take home beers in growlers and cans. Some of their more limited release series are also packaged in 750ml bottles. Distribution plans are in the works to have their beers readily available to the entire East Coast soon.

With all of this great stuff, it'll make you proud to be an American.

HOPKINS ORDINARY ALE WORKS

Hopkins Ordinary Bed and Breakfast, 47 Main St., Sperryville, VA 22740; (540) 987-3383; hopkinsordinary.com/ale-works
Founded: 2014 **Founders:** Sherri Fickel, Kevin Kraditor, David Litaker **Brewers:** David Litaker, Kevin Kraditor **Flagship Beer:** Innkeeper's IPA **Year-Round Beers:** Innkeeper's IPA, Little Devil Blonde, Hazel River Brown Ale **Seasonals/Special Releases:** Saison Noire (each season a new saison is brewed), White Oak Winter Ale, End of the Trail Pale Ale, Appalachian Altbier **Tours:** Upon request **Taproom:** Wed, 4 to 7 p.m.; Sat, 1 to 6 p.m.; contact for special appointment times

You never know where you'll find breweries these days, and that's what makes looking for them a fun, worthwhile adventure. Within the town of Sperryville, Virginia (population approximately 350), there's a historic inn now known as the Hopkins Ordinary Bed & Breakfast. According to the Hopkins Ordinary website, the original brick building was built around 1820, the wood frame portion was added in the mid 1800s, and in the early 1900s once water and electricity were added it became the Sperryville Inn. For a while it was used as four separate apartments until owners Sherri Fickel and Kevin Kraditor bought the building in 2001 and began restoring it to its original use.

Today, not only is it a charming B&B where you can get a wonderful breakfast and a peaceful night's stay after hiking the nearby Appalachian Trail in Shenandoah National Park, but it's also a spot for fresh nanobrewed beer in the cellar downstairs.

As of 2014, the basement space has transformed into Hopkins Ale Works, and beer is flowing from that cellar at the rate of about 1 barrel per week. Guests can get a complimentary tasting or a pint during their stay. Residents can become a member of the brewery and stop by every week or every other week to pick up their pre-paid beer. Different types of memberships are available dependent upon how regularly you want to fill up your growler, and there are special pickup times designated on Wednesday and Saturday.

You can always expect 3 standard beers on tap. This beer is only sold from the tasting room—it's not distributed anywhere else. One of the beers might be the **Innkeeper's IPA**, described as a "modestly hoppy, almost sessionable pale ale." You should always expect a seasonal beer or two. That might be something stronger and a little less sessionable too, like the **White Oak Winter Ale**, a 7.3% ABV holiday beer with hints of ginger and orange peel that the Hopkins team released just before Christmas. Co-founder Sherri Fickel informs me that the "beers are made primarily with barley that is grown in Virginia and malted right here in Sperryville, with some local hops, local honey and other local additives when available and appropriate."

Local ingredients and a local community feel.

Little Devil Blonde
Style: Blonde Ale
ABV: 4.7%
Availability: Year-round on
    tap
Their most popular beer among locals and their Bed and Breakfast Inn guests, this beer is a Belgian blonde ale style that's full of flavor while also lighter in alcohol, proving that just because a beer is considered sessionable doesn't mean it has to be flavorless.

LOST RHINO BREWING COMPANY

21730 Red Rum Dr., Suite 142, Ashburn, VA 20147; (571) 291-2083; lostrhino.com;
@LostRhino

Founded: 2011 **Founders:** Favio Garcia, Matt Hagerman **Brewer:** Favio Garcia **Flagship Beers:** Rhino Chasers Pilsner, New River Pale Ale, Face Plant IPA **Year-Round Beers:** Rhino Chasers Pilsner, New River Pale Ale, Face Plant IPA, Final Glide Hefeweizen, Tmavy Dark Czech Lager, Meridian Kölsch **Seasonals/Special Releases:** Bone Dusters, Maibock Lager, Woody Stout, Dawn Patrol, Cucumber Saison, West Coast Refuge (see website for others) **Tours:** Sat, 1 to 5 p.m. **Taproom:** Tues, 4 to 9 p.m.; Wed and Thurs, 11:30 a.m. to 9 p.m.; Fri and Sat, 11:30 a.m. to 11 p.m.; Sun, 12 to 5 p.m.

When your life revolves around making beer, but you're tasked with following someone else's vision for the beer you make, there often comes a point when you desire that next big, important step: starting your own brewery. Matt Hagerman and Favio Garcia were two of those brewers, who met early in their brewing careers while they both worked at Old Dominion Brewing Company, and realized after years of working for other breweries that it was about time they start their own.

While going on road trips together to beer conferences, meetings, and other types of brewers' events, they began strategizing as to how to put their brewery plan into action. A trip to California was a key turning point, and once back home, they put their plans into action to create Lost Rhino Brewing Company and to replicate a "California tasting room feel that didn't really exist here," co-owner Favio Garcia shared with me.

Home Turf

Style: Farmhouse Sour/Wild Ale

ABV: 7%

Availability: Limited release, Genius Loci Series, in bottles

When you cultivate yeast in house, you can also offer some unique beer offerings that are impossible to get with regular yeast strains. This farmhouse wild beer has a big burst of tartness that's typical of sour beers, with a beautiful orange/golden color. You will either absolutely love this beer or absolutely hate it, but it's worth experiencing either way. Packed with citrus, fruity and sour deliciousness, it's meant to be bold.

Enter the tasting room and you'll find picnic-style tables, a bar—made from a crate that the brew equipment was delivered in—and an incredible, laid-back feel, perfect for an afternoon or happy hour out. A food menu of housemade pickles and nuts, nachos, panini sandwiches, and other tasty bar food is available.

What's not immediately clear at first glance is just how massive Lost Rhino Brewing Company's production facility has become since they opened in 2011, and for those who experienced Lost Rhino from its beginnings, just how much has changed.

In addition to the tasting room, there's a sprawling brew space, where those interested can come in for a tour at designated times on Saturday. To the left of the tasting room, there are more seating areas. Keep walking and you'll find another open room, at least three times the size of the tasting room, which includes another bar and a stage for occasional live music events. Since they opened, they gradually kept expanding until they expanded as much as they possibly could at their current location. New expansion plans are already in progress to add a second location, a brewpub and restaurant in the town of Brambleton, coming soon (by the time you read this it will probably be open)!

When you learn that the Lost Rhino name comes from a surfing term, "someone out to find the best waves, an adventurer," you'll better understand the Lost Rhino beer. Favio is that adventurer, a beer adventurer in a sense considering how he experiments and produces an array of styles. The Lost Rhino team now includes a brewery scientist, who cultivates the yeast in house. Try a traditional German-style beer like the **Rhino Chasers Pilsner**, a crisp, refreshing golden lager, the **Tmavy**, a dark Czech lager at 6.2% ABV (see the Brew Your Own Beer chapter, where Favio has generously shared the recipe and scaled it down to a 5-gallon batch, so you can try to make the Tmavy beer clone at home for yourself), or maybe the **Woody Stout**, a toasty bourbon barrel–aged stout.

OCELOT BREWING COMPANY

23600 Overland Dr., #180, Dulles, VA 20166; (703) 665-2146; ocelotbrewing.com
Founded: 2015 **Founders:** Adrien Widman, Sebastian Widman, Erik Zaber **Brewer:** Adrien Widman **Flagship Beer:** N/A **Year-Round Beers:** N/A **Seasonals/Special Releases:** N/A (all beers are rotating) **Tours:** Upon request **Taproom:** Thurs and Fri, 3 to 9 p.m.; Sat, 11 a.m. to 9 p.m.; Sun, 11 a.m. to 5 p.m.

The stainless steel brew tanks at Ocelot Brewing Company may look the same as any other ordinary brewing tanks, but when you walk back into the middle of the brewery, you'll notice that each one is unique; every tank has its own name. From the brewery side, you can see the names visibly noted on each: names like Jim, Jeff, Jerry, Roger, and Trey.

You may be able to guess who the tanks are named after when you understand Ocelot's theme. Music and beer are intertwined at this brewery. Their logo is a guitar pick, their brewery name is attributed to a Phish song, and all the beers are named after song lyrics. One wall of the tasting room is a Pink Floyd tribute, but instead of *The Wall*, it's *The Barrel Wall*. Behind the bar, there's a guitar hanging on the wall. That guitar is not just a decorative piece—it's meant to be played. Anyone can play it at their leisure whenever they feel like it.

If you're not a fan of playing in front of a crowd, you might play easier after you enjoy a beer or two on tap, considering they often focus on big, strong beers. Choose from beer like West Coast–style IPAs, imperial stouts, and sour beers. Their business model is designed after their drinking styles, as co-founder Erik Zaber describes. The three founders like to experiment and taste different styles of craft beer, noting that "our tastes and expectations are forever changing, and so are our methods of enjoyment"—therefore their personal preferences for drinking beer are reflected in what they're producing for their customers.

The beers are constantly rotating and showcasing a variety of recipes and techniques—proving how the various combinations of grains, hops, and yeast contribute to a beer's unique flavor. Recent recipes have included beers like the **Lemon Yellow Sun**, an imperial hoppy wheat ale featuring lemon drop hops and the **Tangerine Trees**, packed with lots of citrus and grapefruit juiciness.

Beer Lover's Pick

My Only Friend
Style: Russian Imperial Stout
ABV: 9.0%
Availability: Limited release

Dark, roasty, and full-bodied, this Russian imperial stout's malty smooth aromas and taste match its bold 9% ABV. Consider taking home a growler then pairing this beer with some smoky barbecue ribs, or if you're lucky, there'll be a barbecue food truck stationed outside the tasting room, as there was during my visit.

Based in an industrial office complex in Northern Virginia, Ocelot Brewing will regularly have food trucks. You can expect an open, industrial tasting room with a clear view of the brew tanks exposed at the back of the room. While you're relaxing, listening to music and drinking beer, notice all the great use of wood—they reused and reshaped wood from a 150-year-old house that was torn down to create the bar, tables, and many of the fixtures inside.

Contract Brewing

BELTWAY BREWING COMPANY
22629 Davis Dr., Suite 110, Sterling, VA 20164; (571) 989-BREW; beltwaybrewco.com
Less than 10 miles away from Ocelot Brewing, there's a different kind of brewery that's doing a great service for many other brewers across the state. This is Beltway Brewing, a brewery created by Sten Selliers and "built exclusively as a host for partner brewing, contract brewing and production of private label beers." Beltway has developed a great reputation among brewers throughout the region. Some brewers don't have the capacity to expand at their location. Some can't yet financially afford to make the big investment in brewery equipment. Beltway Brewing offers them an alternative solution.

OLD 690 BREWING COMPANY
15670 Ashbury Church Rd., Purcellville, VA 20132; (540) 668-7023; old690.com
Founded: 2013 **Founders:** Darren and Tammy Gryniuk, Mark and Rhonda Powell, Bob Lundberg **Brewer:** Bob Lundberg **Flagship Beers:** Old 690 Beer **Year-Round Beers:** Old 690 Beer, Angry Neighbor Pale Ale, Bitter Neighbor IPA, Roadside Raspberry Wheat, Old 690 Brown Ale, Old 690 Porter **Seasonals/Special Releases:** Old 690 DIPA, Happy Neighbor, Pumpkin Ale, Ol' Man Winter Ale, Sour Neighbor Peach (Sour Ale), Stoner Point Smoked Ale, Coffee Stout, Vanilla Porter, Whiskey Barrel Porter, Coconut Brown, Belgian Triple **Tours:** Upon request **Taproom:** Fri, 5 to 9 p.m.; Sat, 11 a.m. to 9 p.m.; Sun, 11 a.m. to 6 p.m.

On your first trek to visit Old 690 Brewing Company, you have to frequently repeat to yourself that you are not lost. Keep driving even when it appears like you've taken a wrong turn; the dirt road to get there is all part of the experience,

something you may have experienced if you've visited any small wineries over the years, yet still a rare experience for a brewery, and especially one located in Virginia.

This brewery is one of the brand new farm breweries that you should now expect to see more of in Virginia (Senate Bill 430, passed in 2014, amends the Virginia code and makes it legal to have this kind of place), a brewery that's built on 10 acres of farmland and has even started growing some of their own hop plants.

Once inside, you're greeted by a pleasant, comfy tasting room, where there's free popcorn, good beer, and a vast outside space to play cornhole or for the kids to kick around a soccer ball.

The founding Old 690 partnership is a team of five: two couples, the Gryniuks and the Powells, and Bob Lundberg, a pilot who is now both a pilot and a brewmaster. His previous career experience working in a production brewery led him to a meeting with the Gryniuks and Powells and to a new job brewing the beer for Old 690 Brewery.

Bob's focus is to make delicious beer that fits nicely within the parameters of the beer styles he brews. Because this community is also full of wineries, and therefore wine drinkers, he hopes to appeal to all people and in turn, educate the customers who aren't as familiar with craft beer and haven't experienced everything it has to offer.

Beer Lover's Pick

Angry Neighbor Pale Ale
Style: Pale Ale
ABV: 5.6%
Availability: Year-round
Angry Neighbor is named after a real-life angry neighbor, who wasn't exactly thrilled when Old 690 brewery opened; guess this neighbor isn't a beer lover! Either way, in the customary pale ale style, this amber-colored beer has a nice, balanced taste from the use of traditional malts, while the bitter attributes of hops like Cascade make it an easy, enjoyable beer to drink outside with a view of the countryside or inside at Old 690's tasting room. Pairs nicely with the free popcorn inside.

Try sampling in order from light to dark. Start with the **Old 690 Beer**, a pleasing light-colored blonde beer ideal for the warm summer or spring days outside, then move on to the **Amber Ale**. Next sample the medium brown **Old 690 Brown Ale**, toasty with darker, caramel malts. Follow it all up with the **Old 690 Porter**, a deeper, dark smooth chocolatey and coffee-like blend.

OLD BUST HEAD BREWING COMPANY

7134 Lineweaver Rd., Warrenton, VA 20187; (540) 347-4777; oldbusthead.com;
@OldBustHead
Founded: 2014 **Founders:** Julie and Ike Broaddus, Charles Kling **Brewer:** Charles Kling
Flagship Beer: Bust Head English Pale Ale **Year-Round Beers:** Gold Cup Russian
Imperial Stout, Bust Head English Pale Ale, Vixen Irish Red, Wildcat IPA, Chukker Czech
Pilsner, Shorthorn American Pale Ale, Chinquapin Chestnut Porter, Graffiti House West
Coast IPA **Seasonals/Special Releases:** Virginia Hop Harvest Smoked IPA, Covert
h'Ops Black IPA **Tours:** Wed through Fri, 5 p.m.; Sat, 2, 4 and 6 p.m.; Sun, 1 and 3 p.m.
Taproom: Wed through Fri, 3 to 8 p.m.; Sat, 12 to 8 p.m.; Sun, 12 to 5 p.m.

A commitment to sustainability. A brewery site that's full of history. Oh, and Old Bust Head Brewing Company offers one more important thing: something that readers of this book are all undoubtedly looking for—great beer!

Located in a 30,000-square-foot facility, it's one of the new businesses that is part of a 700-acre plot of land—and community—known as Vint Hill. Vint Hill was once a farm, then a military base as early as 1942. Co-founder Ike Broaddus shares that it was once used as a listening post and intelligence gathering station during World War II, and later used as a research and development base until it was eventually shut down in the 1990s. Today the Vint Hill Economic Development Authority has set out to transform it into a thriving residential and business community; Old Bust Head Brewery now plays a key role within that community.

There's not only great beer here, but there's also plenty of space to produce more and more great beer, a 30-barrel brewhouse and six 60-barrel fermenters, and extra square footage and empty space to add more brew equipment as they decide to increase production.

Along with all the usual brew equipment, there are additional pipes, tanks, and technological measures in place for sustainability. Old Bust Head Brewing took no shortcuts, financial or otherwise, in doing everything in their power to create it, from drilling 18 wells and establishing a geothermal system that powers all the HVAC—plus the two large cooler rooms—for their brewery, to securing heat exchangers that preheat all the water for the dishwashers and bathrooms (eventually hoping to be able to generate enough heat for the brewhouse). A cause close to their heart, this was a necessary and vital personal mission they wanted to accomplish when

they set out to build their brewery from the ground up, the most environmentally friendly brewing operation I have ever seen in all my beer travels.

When you enter the beautifully laid-out tasting room, you'll see a long walnut bar—walnut that was cut and refined from the Broaddus's farm—and lots of seating space at wooden tables. Original 1950s columns give it a rustic look in the otherwise new and modern tasting room atmosphere. At the bar, you can place your order of sample trays, pints, and growlers to go. If you're looking for take-out beer in a larger size than 64 ounces, you can also buy kegs, at a separate station near the main entrance. A gift shop in the back corner of the tasting room leads to a back door exit where there's regularly a food truck stationed during tasting room hours.

Brewmaster and part-owner Charles Kling brings his knowledge, experience, and expertise to this craft beer operation, having won numerous awards at the Great American Beer Festival during his previous years with other breweries throughout the US.

Charles met up with Ike many years ago, while Ike was the director of the Vint Hill Economic Authority; he was looking for a facility to set up a brewery. When Charles, Ike, and Julie formed a business relationship together, the brewery plans shifted and expanded to what you see today—a much larger brewery operation than originally planned.

Beer Lover's Pick

Graffiti House West Coast IPA
Style: India Pale Ale
ABV: 7.5%
Availability: Year-round on tap, in bottles, also sold in ½ and ⅙ barrels
West Coast–style Mosaic hops contribute the fruity, citrusy, floral notes that take this beer to the next level. Balanced with the standard grains along with a touch of caramel and roasty malts, this beer is one of those IPAs that may convince non-IPA lovers to give the style a second chance.

Each person brings his or her expertise into the company. Charles brews excellent beers and Julie Broaddus often helps in naming them. She tells me she names the beer after "local anecdotes," and the stories and history behind each name are regularly updated on their website and beer menus, like the **Covert h'Ops IPA**, a limited release beer with roasted coffee flavors and a strong hop finish, named after the secret intelligence operators who used to occupy the brewery buildings. Or the **Shorthorn American Pale Ale**, after the Shorthorn cattle breed. This pale ale in the classic style is crisp, clean with a hint of bitterness and sweetness. Another incredibly popular year-round beer is their **Vixen Irish Red**, after a roaming red fox. The beer's deep amber and red hue coloring will make your mouth water when you see it, and fully satisfied when you taste its caramel, roasted smooth flavors.

OLD OX BREWERY
44652 Guilford Dr., Suite 114, Ashburn, VA 20147; (703) 729-8375; oldoxbrewery.com; @oldoxbrewery
Founded: 2014 **Founders:** Chris, Kristin, Mary Ann, and Graham Burns **Brewers:** Kenny Allen, Noah Kowles **Flagship Beers:** Alpha Ox, Golden Ox **Year-Round Beers:** Alpha Ox, Golden Ox, Black Ox **Seasonals/Special Releases:** Oxplorer Series (IPA-style beer), Saison D'Ox, The Oxorcist, Kristin's Passion (Mexican Hot Chocolate Porter) (see website for most recent releases) **Tours:** Sat, 2 and 3 p.m. **Taproom:** Wed through Fri, 4 to 9 p.m.; Sat, 11 a.m. to 9 p.m.; Sun, 11 a.m. to 6 p.m.

After a pleasant morning or afternoon of physical outdoor activity along the Washington & Old Dominion Trail, you will be pleasantly surprised to see a sign pointing to Old Ox Brewery, around the trail's Mile Marker 25: the ideal resting break.

Chris Burns confirms that in their planning and search for the best location to open their own brewery, they "always targeted Loudoun County as the place to open it." Both Chris and his wife, Kristin, call Loudoun County home, while his father Graham and mother Mary Ann also soon plan to make it their new home, as they relocate there for the brewery business.

This philosophy to keep it local carries over into how and where they choose to distribute their beer, as well as in the design of their tasting room. Through their partnership with the Loudoun Arts Council, there will regularly be new artists' work on display throughout the walls of their tasting room and available to purchase. An industrial-looking tasting room fits in nicely with the industrial business complex nearby, while it's also relaxed and the perfect venue for a happy hour beer out after a full day of work. If the tasting room fills up, there's plenty of mismatched furniture including couches and other tables in the adjoining room where the brewery is stationed, and another open, spacious area to enjoy a beer or maybe even play a game of cornhole.

Opening in 2014, Old Ox Brewery is equipped with a 30-barrel brew system, which means plenty of capacity to keep the taps flowing freely, and you can expect an average of 8 beers on tap during your visit. Head brewer Kenny Allen, who comes with many years of experience and a career at places such as Old Dominion Brewing Company, will be working hard to ensure all the customers' beer needs are met. That will include a wide spectrum of beers, ranging from the **Golden Ox**, a medium-bodied Belgian-style golden ale, to the **Alpha Ox**, their session IPA beer packed with four different hops and piney scents (see the Brew Your Own Beer chapter for the 5-gallon recipe to try making this beer at home). An experimental series called the **Oxplorer Series** will showcase other blends of India pale ale styles, while they will also put out seasonal and specialty batches such the **Farmhouse-to-Table Saison**, using locally sourced honey, sage, and rosemary, and beer such as **Kristin's Passion**, a Mexican-style hot chocolate porter infused with cocoa nibs, cinnamon, vanilla bean, and red peppers.

Note: While this piece was being written, Old Ox Brewery was in the process of dealing with a trademark dispute initiated by Red Bull, the energy drink company. Red Bull filed a complaint with the US Patent and Trademark Office and president Chris Burns responded with a forceful letter in February 2015 in defense of his right to keep the Old Ox Brewery name and branding, urging Red Bull to drop their complaint, but at the time of this book's publication no resolution was yet worked out.

Beer Lover's Pick

Black Ox
Style: Rye Porter
ABV: 5.8%
Availability: Year-round on tap
With a dark black color and a nice creamy foam head, this beer is roasty, chocolatey and a little spicy. Caramel and rye malts create the base for this complex dark porter. Coffee drinkers will notice the subtle coffee flavor, so plan to start your day with coffee and end it with the Black Ox.

PORT CITY BREWING COMPANY

3950 Wheeler Ave., Alexandria, VA 22304; (703) 797-2739; portcitybrewing.com; @PortCityBrew
Founded: 2011 **Founders:** Bill and Karen Butcher **Brewer:** Jonathan Reeves **Flagship Beers:** Optimal Wit, Downright Pilsner, Essential Pale Ale, Monumental IPA, Port City Porter **Year-Round Beers:** Same as Flagships **Seasonals/Special Releases:** Oktoberfest, Tidings Ale, Tartan Ale, Derecho Common, Long Black Veil, Maniacal Double IPA, Revival Oyster Stout, Ways & Means, Colossal Anniversary Series **Tours:** Thurs and Fri, 6:30 p.m.; Sat, 1, 2, 3, 4, 5 and 6 p.m.; Sun, 2 and 3 p.m. **Taproom:** Mon through Thurs, 4 to 9 p.m.; Fri, 3 to 10 p.m.; Sat, 12 to 9 p.m.; Sun, 12 to 6 p.m.

Filling a missing gap in the marketplace is usually one of the signs of a success-ful business strategy, especially when that missing gap comes in the form of a brewery. Bill Butcher, co-founder of Port City Brewing (along with his wife, Karen) noticed that there was not a packaging microbrewery in the major metropolitan area of Washington, DC, and after a long career in the wine business, began to notice some similarities between the customers who enjoyed wine and those who enjoyed craft beer. More importantly, he saw that customers treated it "as a very sophisti-cated beverage" and "that craft beer drinkers treat beer with the same respect that people have always treated wine." In 2011, the metropolitan DC area finally got one of its first packaging breweries since Prohibition ended, when Port City Brewing opened for business.

Northern Virginia

Bill and Karen, along with head brewer Jonathan Reeves, developed their beer offerings with a clear focus in mind: producing full-flavored beers that show off all their layers of flavor—while at the same time being easy to drink. Using his expertise in the wine industry as a model, Bill wanted to produce a range of styles and flavors ranging from light and crisp to dark and full bodied.

On the light and crisp side, try the **Optimal Wit**, made with Virginia-grown wheat and spices like coriander and orange peels, a Belgian-style white ale. In the mid-range of the scale, try the **Monumental IPA**, an East Coast IPA with a bold fruity aroma, or the **Essential Pale Ale**. At 5.5% ABV, it is crisp and refreshing, with citrusy American hops added to the brew tanks using their *Hopzooka* contraption.

The Hopzooka is a machine designed especially for dry hopping. It adds the hops

Beer Lover's Pick

Port City Porter
Style: Porter
ABV: 7.2%
Availability: Year-round on tap and in bottles
With a dark chocolate color to match its dark chocolate aromas, this beer is brewed in the traditional porter style and stays true to its attributes, yet it becomes an all-star beer with its rich chocolate and coffee notes and complex layers of malt. It achieves the top of its alcohol range for its style profile at 7.2% ABV.

to the tank through a closed-loop system powered by carbon dioxide. Built to help improve the quality of the beer and lengthen the shelf life without letting oxygen in the tanks, it's currently patent-pending at Port City Brewing.

Get your own picture next to the Hopzooka machine (like co-founder Bill Butcher opposite) during one of the regularly offered tours at the brewery, then stay for a beer at the tasting room after the tour, an open, bright room with blue and white tiled floors. There's a bar and some cocktail tables where you can enjoy your beer, and you can check out their wall of awards they've won in the short couple of years since their opening. They've received praise and medals for their beer at venues such as the Great American Beer Festival, World Beer Championships, and Virginia Craft Brewers Fest.

QUATTRO GOOMBA'S BREWERY

22860 James Monroe Hwy., Aldie, VA 20105; (703) 327-6052; goombabrewery.com
Founded: 2015 **Founders:** David Camden, Jay DeCianno, Adam and Jessica Meyers
Brewers: Brandon Flanigan, Joel Pugh **Flagship Beer:** Rye Not? Double IPA **Year-Round Beers:** Rye Not? Double IPA, Fannie's Your Aunt English Pale Ale, Cake Eater Honey Wheat, Torque Milk Stout (see website for specifics) **Seasonals/Special Releases:** Seasonal Saison (Mangia La Frutta) **Tours:** By appointment **Taproom:** Fri, 12 to 9 p.m.; Sat and Sun, 12 to 6 p.m.

Quattro Goomba's Brewery is an expansion on an already existing family business that started as Quattro Goomba's Winery in 2006, based on the "history of making wine in the DeCianno and Camden families," as co-founder Jay DeCianno shares. With the enactment of the farm brewery act in 2014, the state of Virginia opened the door to allowing an operation like Quattro Goomba's Brewery to exist.

Today, when you turn off Route 15 and ascend the long driveway leading to Quattro Goomba's farm, you'll get your choice of a number of different venues to check out. There's a small rustic wood building for wine tastings and wine purchases, a separate garage/barn that's been converted into a

Sicilian-style pizza shop (often an occasional live music venue too) where you'll see the barrels and wine-making equipment, and another building whose sole purpose is to serve craft beer. European-style beers are one of their focuses, and seasonal saisons like the **Mangia La Frutta**. Plans for brewing some tasty West Coast–style IPAs are also in the works—their flagship beer will be a **Rye Not? Double IPA**.

Regardless of whether you're there for the wine, beer, pizza, or all of the above, this is a venue to see, especially on a warm day when you can sit outside and enjoy the scenic farm views around you. Family friendly and dog friendly (assuming the dog is outside and on a leash), this is a destination, and for those in the Washington, DC, area, a beautiful day trip outside the city.

TIN CANNON BREWING

7679 Limestone Dr., #130, Gainesville, VA 20155; (571) 248-0489; tincannonbrewing.com; @TinCannonBrewCo
Founded: 2014 **Founders:** Aaron Ludwig, John Hilkert **Brewers:** Aaron Ludwig, John Hilkert, Jose Ortiz **Flagship Beers:** Virginia Blonde, Busted Pipe Black IPA **Year-Round Beers:** Virginia Blonde, Busted Pipe Black IPA, Unkel Dunkel, Vaughn's PB Porter, Breakfast of Champions (see website for specifics) **Seasonals/Special Releases:** Gilligan's Island, Honey We're on a Date **Tours:** Upon request during taproom hours **Taproom:** Fri, 4 to 9 p.m.; Sat, 1 to 9 p.m.; Sun, 1 to 8 p.m.

Some focus on making beer the traditional way—sticking with the tried and true tested method of good beer. Some focus on doing everything but the traditional way; in today's craft beer industry, items such as candy, peanut butter, bacon, and habaneros can all be branded as beer ingredients. Aaron and John, the co-owners and brewers of Tin Cannon Brewing, found a way to do both when they blended Aaron's passion for making the traditional styles with John's abstract ideas to form a well-balanced and unique product line.

With their 2-barrel brew system, they crank out as much beer as they can while still working full-time jobs and managing their time with family. That family time often occurs while at the brewery, as their family and honorary families (the friends and other volunteers who have supported them financially and otherwise in getting Tin Cannon LLC set up) all take a part in the operation; you'll often see them behind the bar of the tasting room or bussing tables or washing glasses.

John's wife, Marcy, did all the pallet wood artwork that adorns the walls, and with colors of deep mustard yellows and browns, it has a cozy, welcoming atmosphere paired with an industrial look created by the metals and silver colors used to cover the refrigeration units behind the bar.

Unkel Dunkel
Style: Dunkelweizen
ABV: 4.8%
Availability: Year-round
This wheat beer is both malty and sweet; the taste for me brings back memories of great travel experiences in the Bavaria region of Germany. It has a hazy brown color, a moderate bitterness, and a clean overall balanced character.

Fun beer names often complement the fun and varied beer styles you have to choose from. Talk to John to get the full story behind **Vaughn's PB Porter**, a 7% ABV Porter brewed with creamy peanut butter. If you knew John in college, you might have also known the real Vaughn whom the beer was named after. Or opt for the **Busted Black Pipe IPA**, hoppy, dark and malty, named for an actual pipe that burst when John and Aaron were brewing this recipe together in a home garage. Prepare to be in for a surprise of flavors with the **Breakfast of Champions**, an amber ale with an added bonus of some bacon and chipotle pepper spices.

WILD RUN BREWING COMPANY
3071 Jefferson Davis Hwy., Stafford, VA 22554; (540) 659-3447; wildrunbrewing.com
Founded: 2014 **Founder:** Everett Lovell **Brewer:** Matt King **Flagship Beer:** Sterling Stout **Year-Round Beers:** Sterling Stout, Smash IPA, Ed's Amber, 0311 Pale Ale, Red Ale **Seasonals/Special Releases:** Lawn Mower Ale **Tours:** No **Taproom:** 7 days per week, 8 a.m. to 6 p.m.

I was never much of a camper, but I found something to persuade me to make a return trip to the campground after my visit to Wild Run Brewing. At Aquia Pines Camp Resort in Stafford, Virginia, sitting by the campfire just got a whole lot more exciting, because you can enjoy your freshly brewed beer while you reconnect with nature and breathe in the fresh air, whether that be while you pitch your tent or while you sit in the cozy tasting room surrounded by a wood-burning fire and chat with Everett Lovell, the easygoing owner of Wild Run Brewing Company.

The primary part of Everett's business is his campground, a business he's owned since the mid '80s. The beer part started as a personal homebrewing hobby, then

Beer Lover's Pick

Sterling Stout
Style: Stout
ABV: 5.7%
Availability: Year-round on tap
Its full-bodied, roasty flavor will keep you warm and cozy as you sit around the fire and look out through windows at your scenic surroundings. Smooth, well balanced, with notes of chocolate and coffee.

transitioned into a homebrew shop within the office of the campground. Inside that office today you can get your necessities like toothpaste and flashlights and simultaneously purchase all the grains, hops, and yeast needed to begin your own path into homebrewing.

"The beers we're brewing are all good solid, middle of the road beers . . . nothing tricky or complicated," Everett explains. Through the beer they make on site, he wants to help educate other homebrewers and prove to his customers that making beer does not have to be complicated. He persuades his customers that it's possible to make a great-tasting beer just by following some basic rules. You don't have to spend all your money on 20 different kinds of grains and hops or crazy ingredients to make an outstanding product.

When you sample some of the beers they make at Wild Run Brewing, you can see Everett's approach put into action with beer recipes like the **SMASH IPA**, a crisp-tasting IPA made with only one hop, Sorachi Ace, and one type of base malt. For a more medium-bodied variety with a little more hop bitterness, try the **Ed's Amber Ale**. For the kids, and for a non-alcoholic option, try the homemade root beer that is served from one of the tap lines.

Brewpubs

CAPITOL CITY BREWING COMPANY

The Village at Shirlington, 4001 Campbell Ave., Arlington, VA 22206; (703) 578-3888; capcitybrew.com

Founded: 1992 **Founder:** David von Storch **Brewmaster:** Kristi Mathews Griner
Year-Round Beers: Capital Kölsch, Pale Rider Ale, Amber Waves Ale, Prohibition Porter
Seasonals/Special Releases: 1st Gut Weizenbock, SurvivAle Saison, Lil' Eye Rye IPA, Roggenbier (see website for more)

Playing a central role in Washington, DC's brewery history, Capitol City Brewing has the honored role of being the first brewpub to open in our nation's capital after Prohibition ended, but for quite a few years now its Northern Virginia location has played the primary and most important role in their operation: brewing all the great beer for both the DC and Northern Virginia restaurants.

Kristi Mathews Griner, director of brewing operations, along with lead brewer Matt Ryan and two assistant brewers, are the experts in charge of making all that great beer. Kristi emabarked on her career in the restaurant business at 16 years old, when she began mastering the skills needed for almost every kind of restaurant job, which eventually evolved into work in a brewpub and ultimately a transition into the kind of work she loves best—brewing the beer. Try one of their signature and most popular year-round beer offerings—the **Capitol Kölsch**, a crisp, classic German-style blonde beer—or look for all the rotating, often new, seasonal offerings that Kristi and her team are developing, like a **Roggenbier**, brewed with malted rye and fermented on a hefeweizen yeast, or the **Tripel Double**, a delicious and strong (8.5% ABV) Belgian-style ale that is then hopped like an American double IPA. Brewery tours are offered the last Saturday of every month.

What's ideal about the Capitol City Northern Virginia location is its great corner spot, with lots of outside seating in the summer months in the Shirlington Village, a shopping and dining complex in Arlington. Inside, sit at the bar where the tanks are front and center. You are guaranteed to get a fresh beer directly from the tanks. Doesn't get much better than that.

MAD FOX BREWING COMPANY
444 West Broad St., Suite I, Falls Church, VA 22046; (703) 942-6840; madfoxbrewing.com
Founded: 2010 **Founders:** Bill and Beth Madden, Rick Garvin, Randy Barnette **Brewers:** Bill Madden, Brad Hulewicz, Max Courington **Flagship Beer:** Kellerbier Kölsch **Beers:** Rock Star Red Irish Red Ale, St. James Irish Dry Stout, Broad Street IPA, Abbaye des Chutes, Kölsch, Defender American Pale Ale, Gridlock India Pale Lager, Saison DuWha?, Praha Pils, Dingo IPA (see website for current selection and the historical beer list for information on past seasonals and special release beers)

Cologne, Germany, is almost 4,000 miles away from Mad Fox Brewing Company, but that doesn't stop executive brewer Bill Madden and his brewing team—Brad Hulewicz and Max Courington—from making a kölsch beer that tastes exactly like

the kind you'd experience when drinking the famous beer style in old town Cologne. Bill recalls someone once telling him "you can't brew a proper Kölsch outside the shadow of the Dom Cathedral" (Cologne's Gothic, towering Roman Catholic cathedral that defines the city's skyline). Bill found a solution. He ordered a little souvenir of the Dom Cathedral from eBay, and perfectly positioned it on top of the lauter tun, where it sits each and every time they brew a kölsch.

You'll find two styles of Kölsch at Mad Fox: the traditional **Kölsch**, the German-style golden ale that uses authentic kölsch yeast sourced from Germany, and the **Kellerbier Kölsch**, which is the unfiltered version served cellar style, and also a gold winner at the 2011 Great American Beer Festival.

In addition to the kölsch, there are lots of other great beer styles represented at Mad Fox, all aligned with Bill's philosophy of brewing the beer in "broad brush strokes." That includes some delicious flavors of cask ale—there are always three to four real ales available on your visit to Mad Fox—as well as beer styles from countries like Germany, Belgium, and of course the US.

Since Mad Fox opened in 2010, the brewpub has gained a strong reputation and put the family-oriented, established community of Falls Church, Virginia, on a map for beer enthusiasts as a must-see destination.

With the help of some longtime friends like Rick Garvin and Randy Barnette, and other colleagues in the beer business, Bill Madden turned his vision for a brewpub into a reality. He established Mad Fox Brewing Company—its name acquired from a combination of his last name Madden and his wife Beth's maiden name of Fox—with the goal of creating a Euro gastropub atmosphere.

You'll realize that was a tough thing to do when you see the exterior of the building, a modern glass building on a straight, heavily trafficked street, not at all like a historic European pub in a 400-year-old building on a narrow, winding street. Step inside and reflect on the smart use of warm wall colors like burgundy, mustard yellow, and deep green, then sit down and look around at all the wood-trimmed bar furniture that transforms the interior space. After a beer or two, you might just believe you are at one of those historic pubs in Europe.

The spacious brewpub—over 12,000 square feet—has three different sections, making customers comfortable whether they are on an outing with their families or socializing among friends while sitting at the bar. There's a dining room, a saloon room, and a pub section. Within the pub space, there is a 63-foot-long bar, which usually means that you have a better chance of finding a coveted bar seat while you choose from a selection of 10 to 12 drafts and a couple of cask ales.

Locally sourced food made from scratch is designed to complement the vast beer selection, ranging from gourmet pizzas to a variety of burgers and sandwiches, to entrees like the Drunken Pork Chop brined with IPA and the Coconut Cod flavored with coconut kölsch.

Look out for a second Mad Fox location in nearby Washington, DC, in the coming months, where they've converted a 150-year-old building—full of its own intricacies—into a cozy taproom. More importantly, admire the fact that all this fresh beer you're drinking in the nation's capital will come directly from the original location, this beautiful 15-barrel brewhouse and brewpub based in Northern Virginia.

MAD HORSE BREWPUB

34 E. Broad Way, Lovettsville, VA 20180; (570) 436-0669; madhorsebrewpub.com
Founded: 2012 **Founder:** Scott Young (current owners David Ratliff and Michael Stephenson) **Brewers:** David Ratliff and Michael Stephenson **Year-Round Beers:** Hefrageous Hefeweizen, Lovettsville Ale, Mad Horse IPA, Just Us Lager **Seasonals/Special Releases:** Hoptoberfest IPA, Mad Horse Chardonnay, Bourbon Stout, Belgian Saison, Maple Bacon Porter

The word "pub" is used broadly nowadays in the names of various beer establishments throughout the world, but its roots go back to the public drinking houses in Britain, which were ultimately great gathering places for the community, a place to catch up on news, sports, and local happenings while you sipped on a pint of beer. Mad Horse Brewpub in Lovettsville does the word "pub" justice.

Open since late 2012, the Mad Horse brewpub functions as a meeting place for the community every night of the week. Choose from pub food selections like Bavarian pretzels, mac 'n' cheese, bratwurst, and pork barbecue nachos, and try the homemade stouty beer cheese.

Along with all the homemade food, enjoy fresh craft beer also made in house with a 7-barrel brew system that's tightly squeezed into the kitchen. Try the **Hefrageous Hefeweizen**, a refreshing wheat beer at 4.2% ABV, or maybe the **Baby Maker IPA** on the other end of the spectrum at 7% ABV. Get a tasting tray for $6. Sit at couches by the fire as you drink, eat, and chat with the friendly bartenders and staff. Owners David Ratliff and Michael Stephenson—both veterans of the US Army—have adopted a veteran's theme and are intent on providing every customer the best service available.

Whatever you do, expect a relaxed, enjoyable night at this local community pub.

Beer Bars

GALAXY HUT

2711 Wilson Blvd., Arlington, VA 22201; (703) 525-8646; galaxyhut.com
Draft Beers: 28

Established in 1990, Galaxy Hut was one of the original craft beer bars in this area of Northern Virginia. Owners Lary and Erica Hoffman focus on a rotating lineup of craft beers comprising small batch and hard to find offerings. Food is designed to cure all your cravings: grilled cheese sandwiches, frankfurters, cheese-steaks, and barbecue sandwiches paired with tater tots or totchos (tater tots with melted mozzarella and cheddar cheese on top).

MACDOWELL BREW KITCHEN

202 B Harrison St. SE, Leesburg, VA 20175; (703) 777-BREW; macdowellbrewkitchen.com
Draft Beers: 50 **Bottled/Canned Beers:** 150

The closest body of water to Leesburg, Virginia, is the Potomac River, but the owners of MacDowell Brew Kitchen, Gordon MacDowell and Nils Schnibbe, have somehow figured out a way to make you believe that you're next to the Atlantic or Pacific Ocean instead. The experience of a beach bar (that's in reality quite a distance from any real beaches) paired with a large tap system—50 drafts, all craft beer—make this a one-of-a-kind beer bar establishment. Hidden in the back of the bar is also a small half-barrel brew system where they frequently experiment with some craft beer of their own.

Outdoor fire pits, multiple bars, palm trees, and regular live music throughout the warmer months all add to the allure of this place while you relax with a beer and sink your feet into the sand. Within just 3 years of their opening date they transformed what once was a space used for a custom kitchen business, office suites, a restaurant, and a parking lot into a beer bar and party destination—the place to go in Leesburg for a fun night out—for tourists and locals alike.

SPACEBAR
709 W. Broad St., Falls Church, VA 22043; (703) 992-0777; spcbr.com
Draft Beers: 24

Who doesn't love the taste of a gooey grilled cheese sandwich? At Spacebar there is an entire menu devoted to 20+ kinds of gourmet grilled cheese sandwiches. Add on the tater tots for a complete meal, then wash it all down with one of the 24 craft beer selections, always rotating, and always all North American craft beer. Spacebar was modeled after owner Lary and Erica Hoffman's original location, Galaxy Hut (see above).

WESTOVER MARKET

5863 Washington Blvd., Arlington, VA 22205; (703) 536-5040; westovermarket.com
Draft Beers: 10 inside, 6 outside in the beer garden **Bottled Beers:** 1,000+ (sold in the market, available for off-premises consumption)

Since 2005, the Hicks family has owned this market that's been transformed into a beer heaven within the community of Arlington. The market has been here since the 1940s, a grocery store but not a destination like it is today; there's still a large variety of groceries, as well as a full-service butcher shop and a Great Wall of Beer that stocks over 1,000 different bottles. Go around the side door or weave your way through the grocery store inside and you'll find an inside bar—almost hidden for those who are unaware of it—as well as an outside beer garden and small bar, with a food menu filled with items from the butcher shop inside.

The beer side of their business has grown so much that they've decided to expand and open another location in another section of Arlington in the near future. Owner Devin Hicks shared that plans are in the works for a new beer garden—Sehkraft Beer Garden and Haus—featuring a "10 barrel brew haus, Music Venue, on-site Butcher Shop, and a Restaurant."

Richmond

In 1775, Richmond was the stage for Patrick Henry's famous "Give Me Liberty or Give Me Death" speech that helped spark the American Revolution. In 1861, during the Civil War, the city served as the capital for the Confederate States of America. These are only two examples among countless others that could be named, but you get the gist; the city of Richmond has a long, notable history.

Its beer history is surprisingly just as long; talk of brewing in the Richmond area was found in records as early as December 1777. For a more detailed explanation, be sure to check out Lee Graves's recent book, *Richmond Beer, A History of Brewing in the River City*, which provides readers with a remarkable account of Richmond's beer history, its role in the city's everyday life, and a description of the many successful beer businesses that were created here.

Though the Prohibition era destroyed many of the city's beer-focused businesses, the city remained a center for many other businesses. Today it continues to remain a center of commerce, while also offering plenty of cultural events, museums, a range of great outdoor activities to choose from, and an attractive location along the James River.

A thriving brewery culture makes complete sense in a city like this, and many residents and business owners seem to have figured this out—finally!

In 2010, there were only a few select craft beer spots in town. From 2010 on, the number has more than quadrupled, and breweries, brewpubs, and craft beer bar destinations are emerging in all of Richmond's neighborhoods, from quaint shopping and eating centers like Carytown, to neighborhoods that once were dotted with tobacco warehouses and industrial complexes.

If you're in Richmond for a visit, please also read through the Central Virginia chapter, where you can tour some other must-see beer spots, many of which are scenic drives and brewery day trips very close to the city's borders.

Beer was so so atmosphere not great

ARDENT CRAFT ALES

3200 W. Leigh St., Richmond, VA 23230; (804) 359-1605; ardentcraftales.com; @ArdentCraftAles
Founded: 2014 **Founders:** Tom Sullivan, Paul Karns, Kevin O'Leary **Brewer:** Kevin O'Leary **Flagship Beer:** Virginia Common **Year-Round Beers:** Virginia Common, Saison, IPA **Seasonals/Special Releases:** Honey Ginger Ale, Sweet Potato and Sage Autumn Ale, Dark Rye Imperial Stout, Belgian Brown **Tours:** No **Taproom:** Mon to Thurs, 4 to 9 p.m.; Fri, 4 to 10 p.m.; Sat, 12 to 10 p.m.; Sun, 1 p.m. to 8 p.m. (Hours change seasonally; please see website.)

The brewery business is often a collaborative effort, and in founders Tom, Paul, and Kevin's case, it was a true collaborative effort—a homebrewers co-operative group formed in a garage within the Church Hill section of Richmond. Its beginnings were simple, "dudes who wanted to brew on a Sabco (system) in 10-gallon batches," as Tom described, which then transformed into a community of interested people who all wanted to know more about homemade beer. Some days there'd be upwards of 70 or 80 people who'd stop by to sample the beer or watch the process of making it on a Sunday afternoon.

Eventually it was time to take it a step further and develop a business plan, and that's how Ardent Craft Ales was established, with an official opening of June 2014 in the Scott's Addition neighborhood of Richmond. Like the neighborhood, the interior tasting room at Ardent evokes an industrial warehouse style: exposed ducts and beams, concrete floors, and a simple layout complete with lots of wood fixtures throughout. It's open and airy. During the warmer months, the spacious outside beer garden is a venue of choice for many Richmonders to spend an entire afternoon or evening, especially when they have the choice of some refreshing beers to enjoy in the sun, like the **Honey Ginger**, a golden-colored summer ale that uses fresh ginger and local honey—about 300 pounds per batch—to invigorate your taste buds. Or enjoy the delicious combination of spicy and earthy in their **Sweet Potato and Sage Autumn Ale**, a farmhouse-style saison. Year-round beers like the **Virginia Common**, a light-bodied ale-lager hybrid, and the **IPA**, a standard, well-balanced American IPA, cater to non–craft beer lovers and craft beer lovers alike.

Ardent's distribution is currently focused only within the metropolitan Richmond area, so though you can get some of its beers at restaurants throughout the city, the best place to experience it is in the tasting room or the outdoor beer garden, where you'll get it fresh on site, as well as be able to enjoy their exclusive and limited release offerings.

Beer Lover's Pick

Dark Rye: Black Pepper Series
Style: Imperial Stout
ABV: 9.8%
Availability: Limited release
Dark-black in color, this beer has the bold richness of the coffee and malty stout flavors, while the rye added to the beer gives it a crisp, slightly spicy undertone and finish. This is one of the first beers Ardent packed in 750ml bottles—all by hand.

GARDEN GROVE BREWING COMPANY

3445 W. Cary St., Richmond, VA 23221; (804) 918-6158; gardengrovebrewing.com;
@gardengrovebrew

Founded: 2015 **Founder:** Ryan Mitchell and Mike Brandt **Brewer:** Mike Brandt **Year-Round Beers:** None at this time **Seasonals/Special Releases:** All beers are small batch, rotating releases due to nanobrewing setup **Tours:** No **Taproom:** Mon, Tues, Wed, 4 to 10 p.m.; Thurs, 4 p.m. to 11 p.m.; Fri and Sat, 12 p.m. to 2 a.m.; Sun, 12 p.m. to 10 p.m.

Walk through the charming streets of the Carytown neighborhood and you'll find equally charming independent shops and tasty eating and dining options. Many of these retail outlets are housed in small colorful buildings, squeezed in side-by-side, and one of those is an unassuming drinking establishment focused on craft beer—Garden Grove Brewing.

Beer Lover's Pick

Solera Stout
Style: Stout
ABV: 8%
Availability: Limited

Go out to dinner before you visit Garden Grove Brewing, but don't order dessert. Save it for the rich flavors embedded within Garden Grove's Solera Stout, where you will experience notes of chocolate, coffee, and even macaroon.

Breweries come in all sizes, and this brewery has captured the essence of what makes the small nanobrewing operations such a draw. Their 3-barrel brewing system and a few fermenters snugly fit in the back of the building while the tasting room space is comfortable and intimate. A bar to the right of the entrance makes you feel like you're hanging out in a friend's living room, while there are a few couches and barrel-designed tables throughout the rest of the tasting room. No food, but you can purchase a selection of meat and cheese packs like you would at the grocery store, and they'll give you a wood chopping board to lay it all out and share it with your friends.

Pair your salami and cheese with the fruit and spicy layered flavors of Garden Grove's **Farmhouse Saison** beer, or experience the fruity hops and bitterness of its **Southern Hemi IPA**, featuring hops solely from New Zealand and Australia. Co-owners Ryan Mitchell and Mike Brandt are constantly experimenting with beer recipes and flavors to provide their local Richmond community with some delicious craft beer, strongly influenced by both Belgian and British brewing traditions. Brewmaster Mike Brandt's background includes years in the winemaking industry, then additional studies specializing in agricultural science and fermentation at Virginia State University. Fortunately for the Carytown community, he's now on to his next adventure—making beer.

HARDYWOOD PARK CRAFT BREWERY

2408-10 Ownby Ln., Richmond, VA 23220; (804) 420-2420; hardywood.com; @Hardywood
Founded: 2011 **Founders:** Eric McKay, Patrick Murtaugh **Brewer:** Brian Nelson
Flagship Beer: Hardywood Singel **Year-Round Beers:** Hardywood Singel, Hardywood Pils, Hardywood Cream Ale, Hardywood The Great Return **Seasonals/Special Releases:** Hardywood Farmhouse Pumpkin, Hardywood Raspberry Stout, Hardywood Gingerbread Stout, Hardywood Poplar, Hardywood Bourbon Sidamo (see website for all beers) **Tours:** Upon request **Taproom:** Wed to Fri, 4 to 9 p.m.; Sat, 2 to 9 p.m.; Sun, 12 to 6 p.m.

Mastering every type of job in your trade of choice gives you an excellent foundation from which to build a business. Eric and Patrick, co-owners of Hardywood Park Craft Brewery did just that—they mastered their crafts within the craft beer industry. They worked as bartenders. They worked in sales and marketing for a reputable beer distributor in the US. Eric created innovative beer mobile apps and served as a speaker on beer marketing strategy. Patrick completed coursework at the Siebel Institute of Technology in Chicago and at Doemens Academy in Munich, Germany, and then apprenticed for brewers in Germany and in New York. They both served as beer judges. The next logical step was to put all their combined knowledge and skills to the best use; they created Hardywood Park Craft Brewery.

Study the beautiful hand-painted mural that covers one entire tasting room wall and you'll get a visual introduction to the Hardywood story; one section of the

Beer Lover's Pick

Gingerbread Stout
Style: Imperial Milk Stout
ABV: 9.2%
Availability: Early Winter
This beer showcases great Central Virginia products like honey and ginger. It pours a dark chocolate, almost black, color. With flavors of vanilla, milk chocolate, cinnamon, and ginger, it's spicy, rich, and indulgent, with a surprisingly smooth finish for a 9.2% ABV beer. The *Beer Advocate* (beeradvocate.com) staff has given it the highest score possible, a 100 world class rating for style. Enough said.

mural is devoted to a painting of open fields of farm land, behind it a sign that reads "Hardywood Park," named after a sheep station in Australia. Next to the sign is a picture of Eric, Patrick, and David Crawford—a passionate homebrewer at that sheep station—who hosted Eric during an orientation program in Australia in 2001, the spot where they first discovered the joys of craft beer. There are pictures of barrels, brew tanks, customers enjoying a beer, the food trucks stationed outside of their brewery, and their head brewer Brian Nelson making the beer. On the mural are also the words "Integrity" and "Heritage," part of their mission to "become one of the most respected brewers in the United States through integrity in our ingredients and in our business practices, through respect for brewing heritage, and through the inspired creation of extraordinary beers."

It appears that they're definitely living by that mission. They have established a strong reputation for extraordinary beers, including beers like their flagship, the **Hardywood Singel**, a Belgian-style blonde ale. Patrick and Eric tested over 200 different recipes for this abbey ale until they found the perfect one. Then there's the **Raspberry Stout**, with the bold flavors of chocolate and sweet raspberries, a gold medal winner at the 2014 Great American Beer Festival in the American Fruit Beer category. Or opt for a beer in their Barrel Series, like the **Bourbon Cru**, an abbey-style quadrupel aged in bourbon barrels.

Since opening, they've added at least four more 80-barrel fermenters and six more 120-barrel fermenters to create all this great beer. They have expanded operations into a second building next door. They increased their output from around 4,000 barrels to 14,000 barrels in a 3-year span. They've hired a full-time director of quality assurance, a position that you don't regularly see at breweries of their size. On weekends they often have events and various food trucks onsite. On warm days there are hundreds of customers enjoying their beers outside in the parking lot surrounded by food trucks and the smell of freshly brewed beer. With an operation like this, it's no surprise that another expansion is highly likely.

It's an exciting time for the team at Hardywood Park Craft Brewery, and just as exciting for the customers who get to enjoy the final product—excellent craft beer—from a passionate, hard-working team who has mastered the art of their trade.

ISLEY BREWING COMPANY

1715 Summit Ave., Richmond, VA 23230; (804) 716-2132; isleybrewingcompany.com; @IsleyBrewing

Founded: 2012 **Founder:** Michael Isley **Brewers:** Josh Stamps, Aaron Lile **Flagship Beer:** 'The Bribe' Oatmeal Porter **Year-Round Beers:** 'The Bribe' Oatmeal Porter, 'Choosy Mother' Peanut Butter Oatmeal Porter, 'Plain Jane' Belgian White Ale, 'Plain Jane Blueberry' **Seasonals/Special Releases:** Bourbon Barrel Series (Oatmeal Porter and Pumpkin Dubbel)—see website for all seasonals **Tours:** Provided for scheduled private events, at other times may be given upon request (based on staff availability) **Taproom:** Tues to Thurs, 4 to 9 p.m.; Fri, 4 to 10 p.m.; Sat, 12 to 10 p.m.; Sun, 12 to 6 p.m.

Cool! People almost like a beer bar

Your first look at Isley Brewing Company is of its brick industrial storefront with a warm mustard yellow sign displaying its name. It's inviting, a reminder of the industrial past still alive in this area of Richmond known as Scott's Addition. The interior is much larger than you may originally perceive from the exterior, and it fulfills its role as a comfortable spot to enjoy a beer with your friends. Founder Mike Isley's wife, Laura, confirms "we started off small and aim to keep it that way, offering artisanal quality craft beers in an inviting space where you can enjoy yourself with friends and family." A patio during the summer months makes it a great place to enjoy the sun. Bring cards, or play a game of shuffleboard or cornhole. Or create your own game; challenge your friends to a game of naming the ingredients in the beer, because those ingredients could be anything, ranging from peanut butter to oranges to apple juice. Their intent is to "think outside the box every time" with the types of beer they showcase to their customers.

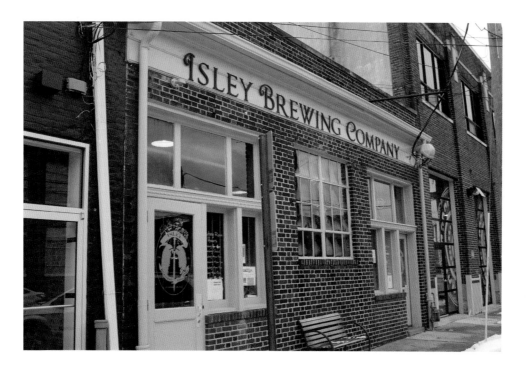

That's beer like the **'Apple Brown Betty' Brown Ale**, which combines the style of the traditional English nut brown ale with some fresh pressed Blue Bee Cider apple juice. Or instead try the orange and chocolate combination in Isley's **'Orange-gasmic' Chocolate Milk Stout**, where you experience the citrusy orange bright flavors with the rich coffee, malty, and milky flavors of a traditional stout beer. Sample

Beer Lover's Pick

'Choosy Mother' Peanut Butter Oatmeal Porter
Style: Oatmeal Porter
ABV: 6.6%
Availability: Year-round on tap

Oats, peanut butter, and chocolatey goodness are stuffed into this oatmeal-style porter, making it smooth and creamy and a beer you'll soon crave just like you would a jar of peanut butter.

both the **'Plain Jane' Belgian White Ale** and the **'Plain Jane Blueberry' Belgian White Ale** side by side to decide whether you prefer the more traditional citrusy light ale or the sweeter version with blueberries.

This section of Richmond is worth checking out if you've never been here before; many of the industrial warehouses that were once here have now been converted to loft-style apartments and other businesses. Isley Brewing is another great addition to the neighborhood.

LEGEND BREWING COMPANY

321 W. 7th St., Richmond, VA 23224; (804) 232-3446; legendbrewing.com; @LegendBrewingCo

Founded: 1994 **Founder:** Tom Martin **Brewer:** John Wampler **Flagship Beers:** Legend Pilsner, Lager, Porter, Brown Ale **Year-Round Beers:** Lager, Pilsner, Porter, Golden IPA, Pale Ale, Hopfest, Brown Ale **Seasonals/Special Releases:** Winter White, Anniversary Imperial Brown Ale, Utebier, Crim Dubbal, Hoovale, Strong Arm Ale **Tours:** Sat, 1 p.m. **Taproom:** Mon to Thurs, 11:30 a.m. to 11 p.m.; Fri to Sat, 11:30 to 12 a.m.; Sun, 11 a.m. to 10 p.m.

[handwritten marginalia: Staple. Solid. Best coffee Stout ever. Food great.]

Many of the breweries in today's Richmond brewing scene are newer businesses, having opened around 2012 or in years following, after the passing of Senate Bill 604 that gave breweries rights to sell their beer on premises without having to have a full service restaurant attached to the brewery.

Then there's a place called Legend Brewing Company, which stands on its own, because it opened approximately 20 years earlier than all the other breweries now in town. Legend's history and story has—to its credit—become a legend in the Richmond community, and after tasting their beer and relaxing on their brewpub deck overlooking Richmond's skyline, with the James River beneath you, you will understand why. More importantly, it should become clear how they've managed to succeed in the ever-evolving craft beer industry.

Their year-round beers are all well-balanced, pleasing beverages that showcase their expertise in creating clean-cut, traditional styles of beer. Try one of their signature flagships like the **Legend Pilsner**, a gold, crisp Bohemian-style pilsner. Or one of their newer seasonal offerings like the **Utebier**, a light, spring ale sweetened by some honey malt and balanced with just the right amount of hops. They are beers that you'll want to drink more than just one of and that may just turn you into one of a group of regular, loyal customers who already frequent Legend's brewpub, at which point you should also add your name to the long waitlist, in order to get coveted access to Legend's limited membership mug club.

The picturesque view from Legend's outside beer garden, a 200-seat deck, is alone worth the experience of visiting Legend, and should be sufficient persuasion to encourage even your non–beer drinking friends to meet there. On colder, rainy days, you can sit inside where you'll discover an airy, open room exposed to lots of sunlight. Among other memorabilia and Legend attire for sale, there are framed pictures of Richmond sights and a canoe hanging from the ceiling, an obvious indication that Legend Brewing and the city of Richmond are inextricably linked.

Beer Lover's Pick

Legend Brown Ale
Style: Brown Ale
ABV: 5.8%
Availability: Year-round
Wonderfully smooth and malty, this British-style brown ale is the most popular beer in Legend's lineup. Caramel, toasted, nutty flavors preside in its full-bodied, complex flavor. Easy to see why it's ranked high up there in the brown ale category among its many fans.

STRANGEWAYS BREWING

2277A Dabney Rd., Richmond, VA 23230; (804) 303-4336; strangewaysbrewing.com; @StrangewaysRVA

Founded: 2013 **Founder:** Neil Burton **Brewer:** Mike Hiller **Flagship Beer:** Albino Monkey White Ale, Woodbooger Belgian-Style Brown Ale **Year-Round Beers:** Albino Monkey White Ale, Woodbooger Belgian-Style Brown Ale, Phantasmic East Coast IPA, Wild Wallonian Dawn Honey Saison Ale, Gwar Blood Hopped Up Red Ale (Nucleus Series) **Seasonals/Special Releases:** Annihilation Series (boldest concoction of beers), Migration Series (seasonal beers), Woodsman Series (barrel-aged beers), Curiosities (uniquely infused small batches), Sours and Wilds **Tours:** Tours offered (call or see website for specifics) **Taproom:** Mon to Thurs, 12 to 10 p.m.; Fri and Sat, 12 p.m. to 12 a.m.; Sun, 12 to 8 p.m.

"Think Strange. Drink Strange" is the Strangeways Brewing motto. When you enter the tasting room, you're also guaranteed to *see* something strange. It's a unique tasting room look.

Bright turquoise-blue and orange paint cover the tasting room walls, along with interesting art spectacles and pictures that you'd expect to see at a modern art exhibit. Sit at the bar and look at the assortment of music and film photographs and beer ads displayed beneath a glass bar top. The monkey is undoubtedly the honorary Strangeways Brewing mascot, represented on everything from the tap handles to a giant monkey statue on the bar wearing a maître d' suit and serving a giant 32-ounce Strangeways can.

Beer Lover's Pick

Oscillate Wildly Blueberry Wild
Style: Sour Ale
ABV: 10%
Availability: Limited, part of a specialty series
Aged in oak barrels for over a year, this beer is part of their "Annihilation series." The word *annihilation* says it all. With a surprisingly high ABV for such a sweet and sour, deliciously tasting dark-colored beer, this concoction has the potential to destroy your soberness in a flash of a second.

Purchase your own 32-ounce take-home can filled with any of Strangeways' strange and interesting offerings, focused especially on sour and barrel-aged beers like the **Vatos Muertos**, a stout with agave nectar and spiced with cinnamon and various kinds of chile peppers, all while being aged in Mexican tequila barrels. Before jumping in to the chile concoctions, you might want to start with their signature flagships like the **Albino Monkey White Ale**, a smooth Belgian wheat ale, or the **Woodbooger Belgian-Style Brown Ale** with its caramel and roasted malts.

If the beer and the laid-back vibe aren't enough, there are also plenty of entertainment options like trivia, live music nights, and even pinball and other video games in another secondary bar area in back.

TRIPLE CROSSING BREWING

113 S. Foushee St., Richmond, VA 23220; (804) 308-0475; triplecrossingbeer.com; @TripleCrossing
Founded: 2014 **Founders:** Jeremy Wirtes, Adam Worcester, Scott Jones **Brewer:** Jeremy Wirtes **Flagship Beers:** Falcon Smash, Element 79, Nectar & Knife DIPA, Saison **Year-Round Beers:** Same as flagships **Seasonals/Special Releases:** Liberty or Death Porter, Red Ale **Tours:** No **Taproom:** Tues to Thurs, 4 to 9 p.m.; Fri, 4 to 10 p.m.; Sat, 12 to 10 p.m.; Sun, 1 to 6 p.m.

Friendships often develop over beer, and co-founders Jeremy, Adam, and Scott have experienced this firsthand. Through their shared beer interests, Adam connected his friend Jeremy with his childhood friend Scott and the three put their individual strengths together to form Triple Crossing Brewing Company. Jeremy and Adam have been homebrewing together since 2010, and Scott is an entrepreneur at heart, who confirms as a child he was the "nerdy kid selling lemonade." As an adult, he was absorbing everything he could about the intricacies of running a business and learning firsthand from his entrepreneurial father's small business ventures.

That small business knowledge came in handy for Triple Crossing Brewing, named after an intersection in Richmond, believed to be one of the only cities in the nation with a triple main-line railroad crossing. With a 7-barrel system and approximately 28 barrels of fermentation space, there's always lots of work to do onsite to keep daily business operations moving and the beer brewing. The brewery and tasting room is based in a large exposed brick garage-like industrial spot that's designed to show off the transparency of the brewing operation. Look behind the bar where you can get a clear view of the brewing tanks while you sample some, or all, of the average 9 beers on draft.

Fans of hoppy beers will be happy to learn that Triple Crossing often emphasizes hop-forward beers, including the **Falcon Smash IPA**, double dry-hopped, **Demon Days**, a hoppy red ale, and **The Proposition**, a double IPA made with flavorful hop varieties like Galaxy and Nelson Sauvin. On the other end of the spectrum, they're working hard to master some historic ale styles and farmhouse beers. During their first year in business, they partnered with the St. John's Church Foundation to

Nectar & Knife DIPA
Style: Imperial IPA
ABV: 8%
Availability: Rotating on tap and in bottles

Mosaic and Simcoe hop additions help to create the tropical, citrusy aromas and hop-forward flavor for this strong double India pale ale. The fruity tones create a nice drinkable beer and stop you from experiencing that bitter finish you might associate with other kinds of IPAs.

create a **Liberty or Death Porter**, and during the release they even had an actor playing the role of revolutionary figure Patrick Henry and portraying his famous "Give Me Liberty or Give Me Death" speech.

Located 2 miles away from the historic St. John's Church, Triple Crossing has a desirable location in the heart of downtown Richmond. The brewery is also adjacent to the campus of Virginia Commonwealth University and less than 1 mile from the Virginia State Capitol in downtown Richmond, a walkable route for many; so there's no real excuse to miss out on the full Triple Crossing Brewing beer and tasting room experience while you're in Richmond.

Brewpubs

ANSWER BREWPUB

6008 W. Broad St., Richmond, VA 23230; (804) 282-1248; theanswerbrewpub.com;
@theanswerbrew
Founded: 2014 **Founder:** An Bui **Brewer:** Brandon Tolbert **Beers:** TBD (house
selections plus guest beer drafts—56 tap lines)

A new venture started by the owner of Mekong Restaurant (see Beer Bars section), An Bui has expanded his Vietnamese restaurant-turned-famous-beer-bar to include a brewpub directly next door in the same shopping plaza. The brewpub's name, named for a recurring slogan that they've used at Mekong in past years, says it all—"Beer Is the Answer."

Wide-open and spacious, this brewpub (current occupancy of around 500 people) houses a 5-barrel system where you can drink the beer as fresh as possible, onsite from the serving tanks.

There's no clear-cut beer focus or recipes they're going for, which also means much more creative freedom to change it up as often as they see fit. Head brewer Brandon Tolbert suggested that plans are in the works to brew some great IPAs. That lineup will include West Coast–style IPAs, served fresh onsite after they brew them, fresher than receiving that same kind of IPA shipped from a West Coast brewery. Future plans also include a sour and barrel-aged program.

Compared to other brewpubs that often serve their beer only at the pub, Answer Brewpub will distinguish themselves by carrying a large number of other guest draft selections. There are 56 tap lines! A selection of bar food is available to pair with your beer, including Vietnamese specialty sandwiches, fries, and chicken wings.

Like Mekong Restaurant, which has already achieved recognition nationwide, Answer Brewpub sets themselves apart by researching and finding the best craft beer to serve to their customers, while simultaneously providing those customers with a comfortable and enjoyable environment. It's a simple mission in concept, but one that's often unachievable in practice. By following in the footsteps of the unique beer bar they've already created, Answer Brewpub should easily make a name for itself.

Beer Bars

THE CASK CAFÉ & MARKET
206 S. Robinson St., Richmond, VA 23220; (804) 355-2402; thecaskrva.com;
Draft Beers: 16 **Bottled/Canned Beers:** 20+ unique styles

Cafes are designed for leisurely days out, places where you're encouraged to stay and settle in for a while. That's why the Cask Café is the best name for this beer and wine bar near Richmond's Fan District. The atmosphere's reminiscent of some appealing beer bars I encountered while living in Europe, and what's cooler is that you can find some equally interesting European beer selections too. Local breweries are often showcased, and make sure to order some of the local sausage and cheese platters to go along with your beer.

MEKONG RESTAURANT
6004 W. Broad St., Richmond, VA 23230; (804) 288-8929; mekongisforbeerlovers
.com
Draft Beers: 60 (52 beers, 8 wines) **Bottled/Canned Beers:** 100+

I've explored many beer bars in my lifetime—beer bars throughout the 25+ countries I've traveled throughout Europe as well as some excellent ones in major US cities—so it's rare that I encounter something brand new, something unique about the atmosphere that succeeds in creating a "wow" experience. Until, that is, I traveled to Richmond, Virginia, and drove past gas stations, fast food chains like McDonald's and Taco Bell, then pulled up to a modest, ordinary-looking shopping plaza, stepped inside, and enjoyed dinner and a beer. I was wowed beyond belief.

This is Mekong Restaurant, a Vietnamese restaurant with an overwhelming selection of food options that's been serving up homemade, mouthwatering ethnic food to the Richmond community since the mid-1990s. Quite a few years after its opening, Mekong made a change to its menu. Instead of pairing the Vietnamese food with the standard wines you might expect to see, they paired it with beer. It started with Belgian beer and it grew to other kinds of rare, hard-to-find beer, and today there's a rotating selection of 52 unique beer drafts—European selections and local Virginia craft beer—that will dare to impress any level of beer geek. If you want wine (though I have no idea why you'd choose wine with all this amazing beer), there are an additional 8 tap lines set up for wine.

After tapping one of their new beer selections, An Bui, chief beer officer, poured me a $\sqrt{225}$ **saison** from BFM (Brasserie des Franches-Montagnes), a small craft brewery in Switzerland. For those who aren't beer enthusiasts and don't know BFM, this is a big deal, a highly sought after beer that is not readily available in many beer bars.

Mekong's reputation for seeking out the best craft beer is well known, and the restaurant has been recognized nationally in the media and on notable craft beer sites, such as CraftBeer.Com, where Mekong received one of the highest honors in their Great American Beer Bar competition for 3 consecutive years (2012 through 2014). With a recently changed website domain name to mekongisforbeerlovers.com, you know they're serious about exceptional craft beer.

SOUTHERN RAILWAY TAPHOUSE

111 Virginia St., Richmond, VA 23219; (804) 308-8350; srtaphouse.com;
Draft Beers: 40 **Bottled/Canned Beers:** 100+

If you're a newcomer to Richmond and want to get a fast-tracked understanding of the Richmond beer scene, Southern Railway Taphouse is a great place to start.

Its location is ideal, in the middle of downtown Richmond near business offices and high-rise hotels. They also serve up some tasty American food and more importantly, a substantial selection of Virginia brews.

Richmond—Pub Crawl

With a total walking distance of approximately 1 mile, this pub crawl takes you through a section of downtown Richmond, beginning near the Virginia Commonwealth University (VCU) campus, and following a route directly east to the last beer bar stop in downtown.

Triple Crossing Brewing, 113 S. Foushee St., Richmond, VA 23220; (804) 308-0475; triplecrossingbeer.com. A perfect place to begin your pub crawl, Triple Crossing Brewing Company is a small microbrewery with a casual atmosphere where you can start with a flight or the many varieties of beer served onsite, and brewed in a brewhouse located directly behind the bar.

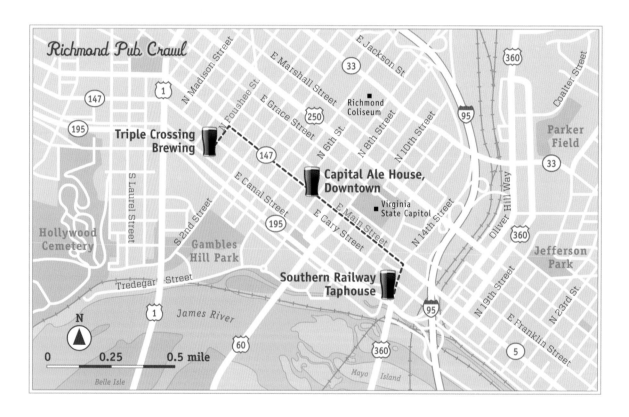

Head northeast on S. Foushee Street toward W. Cary Street (take a right as you exit from Triple Crossing). Continue two blocks until you get to E. Main Street, then take a right, walking almost 7 more blocks until you see Capital Ale House (on the south side of the street). Total walking distance is a little over a half mile.

Capital Ale House, 623 E. Main St., Richmond, VA 23219; (804) 780-ALES; capital alehouse.com. A long bar filled with an overwhelming beer selection awaits you at this second stop, and if you're hungry, you should also grab some food here. Opening in 2002, this beer bar was here long before many other beer bars or breweries in town, and it's in a pretty cool old building too.

Go southeast on E. Main Street (take a right as you exit) toward 7th Street. Turn right onto S. 14th Street. You'll see your final destination on your right (west side of the street) about a half mile down the road. Total walk distance from first to second stop is almost .6 of a mile.

Southern Railway Taphouse, 111 Virginia St., Suite 100, Richmond, VA 23219; (804) 308-8350; srtaphouse.com. At Southern Railway Taphouse, you'll enter to a center bar complete with 40 beer taps with a guaranteed selection of some local Virginia beer. The Taphouse occasionally has events like tap takeovers, poker nights, and live music.

Central Virginia

Not only does Central Virginia include the capital city of Richmond (see Richmond chapter), but it also includes thriving cities like Charlottesville, home to the University of Virginia. Charlottesville has a charming downtown area where you can even plan your own self-guided pub crawl should you want to explore the downtown by foot (see Charlottesville Pub Crawl map).

Travel outside of the Central Virginia cities to find rural communities and farms, where you'll get the opportunity to visit farm breweries like Lickinghole Creek Craft Brewery, built on a 290-acre property in Goochland.

Travel west of Charlottesville toward scenic mountain ranges and stop to admire the views at any number of amazing beer spots, like Blue Mountain Barrel House and Brewery, Wild Wolf Brewing Company, and Devils Backbone Basecamp Brewpub.

Whatever you do, on a trip to Central Virginia, you are guaranteed to have many opportunities to enjoy a diverse array of scenic sights and travel adventures, combined with first-rate beer.

Breweries

APOCALYPSE ALE WORKS
1257 Burnbridge Rd., Forest, VA 24551; (434) 258-8761; endofbadbeer.com; @endofbadbeer
Founded: 2013 **Founders:** Lee and Doug John **Brewers:** Doug John, Jim Knichel, Mike Walsh **Flagship Beers:** Golden Censer, Hoppocalypse **Year-Round Beers:** Golden Censer, Hoppocalypse, Lustful Maiden **Seasonals/Special Releases:** Glorious Dead, Devil's Secret, Cenful Blonde, Barrmageddon, Heavy Red Horseman, 6th Seal, 6th Seal Snack **Tours:** No **Taproom:** Wed and Thurs, 4 to 9 p.m.; Fri, 4 to 11 p.m.; Sat, 12 to 11 p.m.; Sun, 12 to 7 p.m.

As the first craft brewery in Bedford County, Apocalypse Ale Works has ignited interest from the community since it first opened in an old fire station in Forest.

Lee John, co-founder of Apocalypse Ale Works, shared the story of its construction from firehouse to brewery. "This was a community effort. Volunteers helped us with the bar, the ceiling tiles. Local homebrew clubs pitched in to help."

Walk up a ramp to the back entrance to visit the tasting room. Three bars, each with about eight stools each, are stationed throughout the tasting room, a room that used to be the meeting room for the volunteer firefighters. Today this room also functions as a meeting room, only for customers of the brewery instead of the firefighters.

Beer Lover's Pick

Hoppocalypse
Style: Imperial Red Ale
ABV: 8%
Availability: Limited release

The dark amber red color alone lures you to try it, love at first sight. Once you take a sip, the combination of maltiness from the Munich malt and all the aromatic citrus and floral hops is unique, balanced, and full-flavored. You're in for a treat with this imperial red ale.

Outside, you will be happy to discover a large outdoor deck and backyard filled with lots of seating, where customers can also bring their friendly dogs along with them (on leash, of course).

The brewhouse is set up in the front of the old firehouse. Behind the garage doors, instead of fire trucks, there's now a 15-barrel brewhouse and six 30-barrel fermenters, a beautiful sight for Lee and her husband, Doug, to see when they opened the doors to this space in 2013. Doug has been homebrewing for over 25 years. When he began winning national awards for his homebrewing, he knew it was time to start his own business. That began with a homebrew supply store called Pints O' Plenty (which is now in a building next door to Apocalypse Ale Works, see Brew Your Own Beer section) and evolved into a brewery.

His awards didn't stop with homebrewing. Today, the Apocalypse Ale Works brewing team has developed a name for themselves with gold and silver medals in recent years at the US Beer Open, the World Beer Cup, and the Virginia Craft Beer festival. One of those winners was the **Lustful Maiden**, a full-bodied classic Belgian dubbel, as well as the **Heavy Red Horseman**, a Scottish Wee Heavy beer that's a must try for those who embrace all-things-malty. Continue your malty beer journey with the **Barrmageddon**, a Bavarian lager made with some classic German malts and hops.

BLUE MOUNTAIN BARREL HOUSE AND BREWERY 3/27/16 good atmosphere, corn hole, good beer

Brewery Address: 9519 Critzers Shop Rd., Afton, VA 22920; (540) 456-8020
Barrel House Address: 495 Cooperative Way, Arrington, VA 22922; (434) 263-4002; bluemountainbrewery.com; @BlueMtnBrewery
Founded: 2007 **Founders:** Mandi and Taylor Smack **Brewers:** Matt Nucci and Taylor Smack (Brewery); Chad Dean and Joseph Beck (Barrel House) **Flagship Beer:** Full Nelson Virginia Pale Ale **Year-Round Beers:** Full Nelson, Classic Lager, Kölsch 151, Dark Hollow, A Hopwork Orange **Seasonals/Special Releases:** Blue Reserve, Mandolin, Rockfish Wheat, Evil 8, 13.5 Oktoberfest, MacHayden's Wee Heavy, Evan Altmighty, Maggie Maibock **Tours:** Sat., 12 to 4 p.m. **Taproom:** Barrel House winter hours—Mon, Wed, and Thurs, 11 a.m. to 6 p.m.; Tues, Fri, and Sun, 11 a.m. to 8 p.m.; Barrel House hours (starting Apr. 1st)—Sun to Thurs, 11 a.m. to 8 p.m., Fri and Sat, 11 a.m. to 9 p.m.; Brewery hours— Mon to Sat, 11 a.m. to 10 p.m.; Sun, 11 a.m. to 9 p.m.

Blue Mountain Brewery: In the mid 2000s, Taylor and Mandi Smack, husband and wife team and co-founders of Blue Mountain Brewery, journeyed down the challenging path of opening their own brewpub. Their location choice was genius— Nelson County's Route 151, an area filled with wineries, where tourists and tour buses frequented and where local Virginians explored. Mandi and Taylor explored

it often during their days off, traveling from Charlottesville to Route 151, visiting the wineries and admiring the gorgeous views from the base of the Blue Ridge Mountains. Yet they knew there was something clearly missing. You may have guessed what that was—beer.

They bought land, built a small house, started growing their own hops, and then built their brewpub called Blue Mountain Brewery in Afton.

When the brewpub opened in 2007, there was no outside seating and there was a simple, functional setup of about eight long communal-style picnic tables for seating inside. Today they can accommodate large parties and seat hundreds of people outside on their stone patio and outdoor beer garden overlooking the Blue Ridge Mountains (there's even a separate area that's dog friendly for those guests who want to bring their pet along on a leash).

Along with a customer-pleasing outdoor beer garden, there's now a decent-sized seating area inside, along with a 15-barrel brewhouse, a quality food menu, and a separate event space they use for large groups, like weddings, corporate events, and bus tours that visit the Route 151 attractions.

On the Blue Mountain website, you'll see the slogan, "Nelson County's Original Craft Brewery." That's because today they're not the only brewery along Route 151 in Nelson County. Soon after they opened, other brewpub businesses followed suit, including Devils Backbone Basecamp Brewpub and Wild Wolf Brewery, and today

Beer Lover's Pick

Full Nelson Virginia Pale Ale
Style: Pale Ale
ABV: 5.9%
Availability: Year-round on tap and in bottles
This beer succeeds in creating a great balance between the traditional pale ale and the extra-hoppy IPA styles. Citrusy, spicy, and slightly earthy aromatic hops achieve a bittering hop bite, while its medium-bodied, amber color, and English ale attributes create an interesting and pleasing maltiness. Cool tidbit to note: They use the hops grown from their own farm for this beer!

there's also a cidery, a distillery, and seven other wineries. It's a destination, regardless of your alcoholic beverage of choice.

Blue Mountain Barrel House: In 2012 they expanded and opened the 30-barrel Blue Mountain Barrel House, 26 miles south in Arrington, to meet their increasing beer demand. They are already very close to reaching their maximum brewing capacity of about 15,000 barrels per year. The Barrel House doesn't serve food, but has a spacious onsite tasting room and a mezzanine on the second floor with darts and foosball where you can get a front row seat to watch the brewers in action. Both facilities offer the most amazing views of the surrounding countryside and mountains.

Views might be what you come in for, but you'll stay for the beer. That beer includes the **Dark Hollow**, an imperial stout aged in American bourbon barrels, available all year round. Hop lovers might try one of their newer offerings, **A Hopwork Orange**, a 7% ABV orange-infused IPA that uses natural oranges to create a burst of citrus deliciousness. On a warm spring day outside in the beer garden, enjoy the **Rockfish Wheat**, a Bavarian-style hefeweizen with a subtle, sweet banana undertone.

CENTER OF THE UNIVERSE BREWING COMPANY

11293 Air Park Rd., Ashland, VA 23005; (804) 368-0299; cotubrewing.com; @COTUBrew
Founded: 2014 **Founders:** Chris and Phil Ray **Brewer:** Mike Killelea **Flagship Beers:** Pocahoptas IPA, Ray Ray's Pale Ale, Main Street **Year-Round Beers:** Pocahoptas IPA, Ray Ray's Pale Ale, Main Street Virginia Ale, Chin Music Amber Lager, Slingshot Kölsch **Seasonals/Special Releases:** Shut Up, Oktoberfest, Scotchtown, Homefront IPA, Monkeys Uncle, El Duderino **Tours:** No **Taproom:** Tues to Fri, 4 to 9 p.m.; Sat, 1 to 9 p.m.; Sun, 1 to 6 p.m.

Scientists and cosmologists may declare that there is no *real* center of the universe but residents of Ashland, Virginia, understand differently. The town of Ashland has labeled itself as the Center of the Universe since reportedly the mid-'80s or so. Then in 2014, Center of the Universe Brewing (COTU) opened, about 5 miles from Ashland's center, named after that funny, unusual town slogan. Part of COTU's philosophy revolves around the idea of "taking pride where you live and respecting the people with whom you interact."

Owners and brothers Chris and Phil Ray have embraced this philosophy and the local community around them from the start. Many of those local residents have signed up for a free-to-join social club that the COTU team has created called the Satellites, where members earn points by visiting the brewery and participating in events that the brewery sets up for the members.

Beer Lover's Pick

Pocahoptas IPA
Style: India Pale Ale
ABV: 6.8%
Availability: Year-round on tap and limited
   amount packaged in 22-ounce bottles

West Coast–style IPAs are well sought after these
days, particularly because it's often difficult to get
some of the hops that are known for being sexy
and full flavored. COTU's IPA is a nice example
of the West Coast–style IPA, unfiltered, wth lots
of great aromas from the four different kinds of
Pacific Northwest hops that are blended together,
sure to satisfy any hophead.

Many of these club members think of it as an extension of their own living room and rightly should—the tasting room is designed with that kind of experience in mind. There's a comfortable main space and bar where families can bring their children along with a bookshelf stacked with games propped up along the wall. There's a separate space in the back with four dartboards and cocktail tables made from barrels, and a roomy outdoor beer garden and patio. It's all based in an industrial park complex, but once you're inside you're in your own kind of universe, with good people, good beer, and good entertainment options.

Satellite members can't wait for special release beers like the **El Duderini**, a White Russian stout that's released in November every year, or popular year-round beers like the **Chin Music**, an amber lager and the official beer of the Richmond Flying Squirrels baseball team.

The baseball theme makes complete sense when you learn that co-owner Chris Ray's prior career was as a Major League Baseball player. Actual Louisville Slugger maple baseball bats are aged in a beer called the **Homefront IPA** released on Memorial Day every year. 100% of the proceeds go to a designated military charity. Today there are 10 craft breweries from the United States participating in this charity effort, an effort called Hops for Heroes that Chris Ray co-founded.

CHAMPION BREWING COMPANY
324 6th St. SE, Charlottesville, VA 22902; (434) 295-2739; championbrewingcompany.com; @championbeer
Founded: 2012 **Founder:** Hunter Smith **Brewers:** Hunter Smith (Head Brewer), Levi Duncan (Lead Brewer), Jon Richards (Pub Brewer), Josh Skinner (Lead Cellarman, Director of Wild Fermentation) **Flagship Beers:** Missile IPA, Killer Kölsch **Year-Round Beers:** Missile IPA, Killer Kölsch, Stickin' in My Rye IPA **Seasonals/Special Releases:** Tart Berliner Weisse, Face Eater Gose, ICBM Double IPA, Fruitbasket Double IPA (see website or call for specifics) **Tours:** No **Taproom:** Mon to Wed, 5 to 9 p.m.; Thur to Fri, 1 to 11 p.m.; Sat, 1 to 11 p.m.; Sun, 1 to 8 p.m.

Venture off the main street in downtown Charlottesville and you'll discover some other great spots worth checking out; Champion Brewing Company's tasting room is one of them, a short walk from the center. The industrial feel inside pairs nicely with Champion's reputation as a local neighborhood spot.

Within a very short time from their opening date in December 2012, they expanded and opened up a production facility outside of downtown, nicknamed The Missile Factory, which houses a 30-barrel system. Larger batches and an increased beer production means they can now distribute their canned beer to a larger area, while also keeping their taproom as intimate and local community oriented as was

Missile IPA

Style: India Pale Ale

ABV: 7%

Availability: Year-Round on tap and in cans

The Missile IPA is representative of that full-balanced American IPA dry-hopped with Simcoe, Cascade, and Summit hops and the right amount of bitterness for lovers of hoppy beers. It was one of the first beers Champion brewed and canned when they opened their larger production facility known as the Missile Factory.

Central Virginia

originally designed. At the taproom and original location, they still brew from their smaller 3-barrel system for pilot batches and to produce some of their experimental beer creations.

During my visit there were 9 different beers on tap. Founder Hunter Smith notes that they are "focused on high-quality and interesting beers, with a penchant for hoppy and sour beers." Beers like the **Killer Kölsch**, a hybrid-style beer, is one of those high-quality beers. It's mildly hopped, refreshing and clean. Then there are the IPAs, like their flagship **Missile IPA** and the **Stickin' in My Rye IPA**, a beer they collaborated on with the legendary punk band NOFX and brewed with some spicy rye and West Coast–style hops. The IPAs don't stop there—you can also choose from double IPA options like the Fruitbasket DIPA and the ICBM Double IPA.

C'VILLE-IAN BREWING CO.
705 W. Main St., Charlottesville, VA 24551; (434) 328-2252; cvillebrewco.com; @CvilleBrewCo
Founded: 2014 **Founder:** Stephen Gibbs **Brewer:** Bill McWood **Flagship Beers:** Albemarle Amber **Year-Round Beers:** Albemarle Amber, Paramount Pale Ale, Pavilion Porter **Seasonals/Special Releases:** C'ville on the Rye'z IPA, Blenheim Brown Ale, Pumpkin Ale **Tours:** No **Taproom:** Tues and Wed, 5 to 10 p.m.; Thurs and Fri, 3 to 11 p.m.; Sat 12 to 11 p.m.; Sun 1 to 8 p.m.

Downtown Charlottesville is a charming town. There are boutiques, local stores, bars, restaurants and now, with the addition of C'ville-ian Brewing in 2014, a nanobrewery, in a narrow downtown building on West Main Street.

Walk in the door to unwind in a simple and homey tasting room, so homey that when I arrived, there was even a dog making himself at home, stretching out on the dark brown leather couch and inspecting every customer who entered. Owner Stephen Gibbs is a veteran of the US Army, and he designed the interior of the tasting room to stick with the American theme: a red-colored bar, white walls, a blue ceiling, and exactly 50 lightbulbs hanging inside. A few beer quotes are written on the walls, like the well known "Beer is proof that God loves us and wants us to be happy," claimed to have been said by Benjamin Franklin.

Next to the couch there is a coffee table lined with magazines and behind that the bar. The brewery equipment is all housed in a smaller contained space at the back of the building.

A nanobrewery is generally defined as a brewery that produces 3 barrels, or a little less than 100 gallons, of beer at one time. As a result of this smaller brew system, head brewer Bill McWood has the freedom to experiment with various types

Albemarle Amber
Style: Amber Ale
ABV: 5.7%
Availability: Year-round on tap
Nice, balanced biscuit graininess and some flavorful hops like the popular Cascade hops and Centennial varieties make this beer a smooth, drinkable ale. A great choice to begin your night out.

of beer, testing out what his customers like and don't like. The lineup includes beers like the **C'ville on the Rye'z IPA**, a golden rye beer with lots of hops, and the **Blenheim Brown Ale**, a traditional Northern English–style ale.

LICKINGHOLE CREEK CRAFT BREWERY

4100 Knolls Point Dr., Goochland, VA 23063; (804) 314-4380; lickingholecreek.com; @LCCB-farmbrews
Founded: 2013 **Founder:** Lisa and Sean-Thomas Pumphrey, Farris Loutfi **Brewer:** Sean-Thomas Pumphrey **Flagship Beer:** Magic Beaver Belgian-Style Pale Ale **Year-Round Beers:** Three Chopt Tripel, 'Til Sunset IPA **Seasonals/Special Releases:** Enlightened Despot, Batchelors Delight, Fearnought Bourbon Barrel Imperial Brown Ale, Nuclear Nugget Imperial Honey IPA (many more listed on website) **Tours:** Private tours by appointment **Taproom Hours:** Refer to website for specifics

With 360-degree views of the stunning Goochland County countryside, you are in for a one-of-a-kind experience on this 290-acre farm brewery. One-of-a-kind isn't exaggerated here; there's no other brewery quite like this within the state of Virginia—at least for the time being.

Co-founders Lisa and Sean-Thomas Pumphrey hope to change that, though, in their big task to set a new "agricultural business model," as Lisa shares, for

themselves and others, with the goal of helping farming businesses flourish and make a living.

Problem is, all this wasn't a legal thing to do, until just recently. Wineries can do it, but breweries have different laws, so before Lisa and Sean-Thomas could create their farm brewery, they needed to change the law. To do that, they worked with the county for an ordinance change and spent countless hours lobbying local and state officials. In 2014, their work paid off. Senate Bill 430 passed in the state of Virginia. Lickinghole Creek Craft Brewery could finally open.

On this farm, the main attraction is the beer, and to make that beer, you need some basic ingredients. Lisa and Sean-Thomas's hope is that one day all of these basic ingredients can come from their farm, instead of relying on outside suppliers.

As early as 2007, years before they started the brewery, they planted some hops in the ground. Then in 2013, they added more hops to their hop yard—twelve 100-foot rows of Columbus, ten 200-foot rows of Cascade, and six 200-foot rows of Nugget.

Another base ingredient is the malted barley. They've planted 13 acres of Thoroughbred Barley, and started to introduce wheat and rye this year. Lisa noted that "certain beers have the malt we actually brew here."

Plants and herb gardens that the Lickinghole Creek Craft Brewing team has developed on their land, under consultation and with the support from Backyard Farmers, will complement the base flavors of the beer. This includes herb gardens, blueberry bushes, fig trees, and orange trees.

When you visit, your route will take you on some winding roads, followed by a long gravel road leading up to the brewery. The brewery is in a 4,100-square-foot building on top of the hill, resembling a horse barn and blending in with the landscape, like it was always meant to be there.

Mark your calendar for some of their events, like their beer release parties on the grounds. The release of their **Fearnought Bourbon Barrel Imperial Brown Ale**, aged in Kentucky bourbon barrels, was timed perfectly to coincide with the Kentucky Derby. During the event, held in support of the Thoroughbred Retirement Foundation's James River chapter, they held special activities on the grounds like pony rides, live music, and Best Dressed and Best Hat contests.

On other days that the tasting room opens, order your beer inside where you can see all the shiny brew tanks, then go back outside to admire the views around you. In the winter, heated tents are set up outside, and in the summer you have all the open space you can possibly need to move around, admire the views, and enjoy your beer at the same time.

You can even take a hike on their land if you want to get some exercise after the beer. There's not really anything that classifies as light beer for those counting the calories, nor was it meant to be light. Most of their recipes are strong and bold. All are delicious.

La Calvera Catrina
Style: Belgian Tripel
ABV: 11.3%
Availability: Limited release

You'll never think the same way about tequila after you taste this beer, because though you taste the potent tequila flavors (this beer was aged in Mexican tequila barrels for over 3 months), you get a complexity of other flavors that really shine and take the spotlight: lime zest, citrus notes, and sweetness all at once. The base of this beer is their Three Chopt Belgian Tripel recipe, a beer that's already won some rave reviews among beer geeks.

With a name like Lickinghole Creek (named after a creek that runs through their property, by the way), there have to be equally inventive names for the beer. There are.

Try the **Enlightened Despot**, a bourbon barrel Russian imperial stout, made with 10 specialty grains, American hops, and aged in 15-year-old wheat bourbon barrels. This beer also got them 94 points out of a highest possible ranking of 100 from the *Beer Advocate* "Bros" (the two founders who own and operate the website). Among other rave reviews, they described the beer as "something to savor."

Or attempt to analyze the combination of strong, spicy, and sweet flavors you're tasting as you sample the **Redneck Soap Opera**, described on Lickinghole's website as a "rum barrel aged spiced Belgian-style Quadruple Ale." Needless to say this is another big and bold beer, in both flavor and ABV amount (11.5% ABV).

For a lighter in alcohol option, enjoy a pint of the **Magic Beaver Belgian-Style Pale Ale** that uses Belgian yeast and pilsner malt or the **'Til Sunset** Session IPA.

While you enjoy the **'Til Sunset**, you should plan on staying for the sunset. You won't regret it.

MIDNIGHT BREWERY

2410 Granite Ridge Rd., Rockville, VA 23146; (804) 356-9379; midnight-brewery
.com; @MidnightBrewery
Founded: 2011 **Founder:** Trae Cairns **Brewers:** Trae Cairns, Becky Rudolf **Flagship
Beer:** Rockville Red **Year-Round Beers:** Not My Job, Rockville Red, New Beginning,
Head First, Purdy Mechanic, Midnight Granite **Seasonals/Special Releases:** Cairns Wee
Heavy, Virginia Midway **Tours:** Upon request **Taproom:** Tues to Thurs, 4 to 8 p.m.; Fri, 4
to 9 p.m.; Sat, 1 to 8 p.m.; Sun, 1 to 6 p.m.

Having the full support of your family and community is important when you're
taking a major career risk. Trae Cairns, founder of Midnight Brewery, fortunately had that kind of support in the process of starting his own brewery, most
importantly from his wife, Debra, who urged him to go after his dream career after
over 8 years homebrewing more and more frequently. Other forms of support came
from volunteers who worked, and still work, in the tasting room, and even volunteers like Becky Rudolf, lead brewer, who volunteered to brew until the time when
Trae could afford to put her on the payroll. Trae's mom even learned a new job to
offer her support for her son's business; she became the unofficial keg-washer.

Rockville Red
Style: Irish Red Ale
ABV: 5.5%
Availability: Year-round on tap
Midnight Brewery's flagship beer, the Rockville Red is the epitome of a balanced, delicious sessionable beer. Malty with hints of caramel, it's a nice beer to enjoy in Midnight's comfortable tasting room with your friends.

That's why it was important that the location of the brewery also be close to home, close to the community where Trae grew up—hence the brewery's slogan, "Virginia Born and Raised." A self-funded brewery business is not common in today's craft beer industry, especially when you understand the major investment costs for the brewing systems and the large capacity of fermentation tanks you need to get things running.

Trae's goal was for it to be fully self-funded, which meant that Midnight Brewery started small—while Trae was still working full-time at his information technology job—on a 1.5-barrel brewing system in a 1,250-square-foot building. As the business grew, and equipment was paid off, he focused on adding new equipment.

Today, Midnight Brewery is in a building more than four times the size of the original building, with a 10-barrel system and 20-barrel fermentation tanks. The beer is brewed with a focus on balanced, sessionable beers, like the **Not My Job,** a Southern English–style brown ale that's malty with a subtle touch of sweetness. Whether or not you're an IPA fan, you should still plan on trying a sample of the Midnight's **Purdy Mechanic**, a more sessionable West Coast–style IPA at 6% ABV. Or try the **New Beginning**, a light kölsch-style beer made with pilsner malt. When you head to the Midnight Brewery tasting room and sip on the refreshing **New Beginning**, you might remember that everyone has the chance for a new beginning if they so choose. Trae Cairns is one of those guys who can prove he got his, and share his story for inspiration if you need it.

RUSTY BEAVER BREWERY

18043 Jefferson Davis Hwy., Ruther Glen, VA 22546; (855) 478-7892; rustybeaverbrewery.com; @RustyBeaverBrew

Founded: 2013 **Founders:** Rick and Austin Ivey **Brewer:** Austin Ivey **Flagship Beer:** Buck Tooth "Big Bite" IPA **Year-Round Beers:** Buck Tooth "Big Bite" IPA, Roy's Big Bad Brown Ale, Smashed Bastard, Quake Stout **Seasonals/Special Releases:** Peter Pumkin Eater, Merry Krampus Spiced Porter, Top Down Summer Ale, Amazing DIPA Brothers, Fugged Up Amber Ale **Tours:** No **Taproom:** Mon to Thurs, 4 to 8 p.m.; Fri and Sat, 12 to 9 p.m.; Sun, 12 to 6 p.m.

good Beer Random location

Austin Ivey, brewmaster and co-founder of Rusty Beaver Brewery along with his dad, Rick, loves his job as brewer. He makes beer. He also makes cheese. Their location, in the middle of a shopping plaza near a Food Lion grocery store, was not their first choice when they started the planning process for their brewery, but it serves its purpose.

It allows them to make beer, serve great local customers, and easily travel back and forth to the 30-acre family farm. The Rusty Beaver team has made the most of their space, filling it with a 3-barrel brew system along with some 5-barrel holding tanks. There's a couch and a few tables for customer seating upon entering, and a bar in the middle. Stop in after a day of errands around town and try fresh-brewed beer like the **Buck Tooth "Big Bite" IPA**, a 7.5% ABV beer packed with hops, or maybe opt for something lighter like the **Smashed Bastard**, smashed standing for a single malt and single hopped beer, making it smooth, crisp, and refreshing at a more sessionable 5.2% ABV.

Beer Lover's Pick

Roy's Big Bad Brown Ale

Style: Brown Ale

ABV: 5.7%

Availability: Year-round on tap

This malty brown ale has some great richness and caramel and chocolate notes. It's exactly what you anticipate tasting if you're hoping for that traditional brown ale flavor profile, and pours a deep brown, almost black, color.

Central Virginia

STARR HILL BREWERY

5391 Three Notched Rd., Crozet, VA 22932; (434) 823-5671; starrhill.com; @StarrHill

Founded: 1999 **Founders:** Mark Thompson and Kristin Dolan (current president/CEO is Brian McNelis) **Brewer:** Robbie O'Cain **Flagship Beer:** Northern Lights IPA, Grateful Pale Ale **Year-Round Beers:** Northern Lights IPA, Grateful Pale Ale, The Love Wheat Beer, Jomo Vienna Lager, Double Platinum Imperial IPA **Seasonals/Special Releases:** Reviver, Soul Shine, Boxcarr, Snow Blind, Shakedown, Sabbath, King of Hop, White Shade of Pale Ale (see website for specifics) **Tours:** Sat and Sun, 1, 2, 3, and 4 p.m. **Taproom:** Wed to Fri, 12 to 8 p.m.; Sat, 11 a.m. to 8 p.m.; Sun, 12 to 6 p.m.

Named Starr Hill because it originally opened in downtown Charlottesville, sharing its spot with the legendary Starr Music Hall, the brewery grew from a small craft brewery operation to what it is today, a large production facility producing approximately 28,000 barrels per year, distributing its beer throughout the Mid-Atlantic and Southeast region to places like Virginia, Delaware, Georgia, Maryland, North Carolina, Pennsylvania, Tennessee, Washington, DC, and its newest territory, northern and central Alabama.

Since 2005, they've been based at their current location in Crozet, offering some cool regular events and nights out to support their local community. One of those is a Cheers For Charity monthly fundraiser, where $1 from every pint sold on those nights at the taproom will go to a designated local Charlottesville area nonprofit group. There's fun meet-ups like a Ladies Night, when there's often live music; a

recent band played '90s girl rock music from famous musicians like Jewel and Alanis Morissette. When there's a major University of Virginia sporting event on TV, the tasting room often transforms into a lively sports bar.

Industrial and spacious, the tasting room is decorated in silver and wood brown-colored fixtures. One wall is plastered with a myriad of posters from past concerts and live music events that Starr Hill has hosted or participated in. The bright red Starr Hill tap handles stand out, luring you in to try one (or more) of the 16 beers that you'll find on tap. During warmer months, you can sit outside on the tasting room's patio, at which point you should definitely sample one of their year-round beer selections like **The Love Wheat Beer**, an unfiltered German hefeweizen style.

Other beer options include their signature year-round selections like the **Northern Lights**, a full-flavored American India pale ale, or the **Dark Starr Stout**, their most awarded beer, a robust Irish dry stout that's rich and complex from the roasted barley and coffee notes.

Brewmaster Robbie O'Cain is now continuing the tradition of some of those earlier great Starr Hill recipes (recipes invented by the original founder, Mark Thompson, who has since retired), as well as contributing his own great recipes to carry Starr Hill forward into the future of Virginia craft beer. According to the brewery website, since Robbie joined Starr Hill in 2011, his leadership skills and contributions to brand and recipe development have helped Starr Hill win awards for some of their newer beers including the **White Shade of Pale Ale** and the **King of Hop Imperial IPA.**

With so many new breweries, Starr Hill Brewery is one of the originals, one that has a long-standing reputation in the Charlottesville and Central Virginia region. Stop by the tasting room to see it and enjoy it for yourself.

Beer Lover's Pick

Grateful Pale Ale
Style: Pale Ale
ABV: 4.7%
Availability: Year-round
This is a pleasant, light-bodied pale ale with citrusy aromas and flavors from the hops. Its malt base is smooth and adds some pleasing caramel and toast notes.

THREE NOTCH'D BREWING

946 Grady Ave., Charlottesville, VA 22903; (434) 293-0610; threenotchdbrewing .com; @ThreeNotchdBeer

Founded: 2013 **Founders:** Scott Roth, George Kastendike, Derek Naughton **Brewer:** Dave Warwick **Flagship Beers:** 40-Mile IPA, Hydraulion Red **Year-Round Beers:** 40-Mile IPA, Hydraulion Red, The Ghost, No Veto **Seasonals/Special Releases:** Farmers Pale Ale, Hansel and Kettle Imperial Oktoberfest, Biggie Smores Imperial Stout (see website for full list) **Tours:** Sat, 2 p.m. **Taproom:** Tues to Thurs, 4 to 10 p.m.; Fri, 3 to 11 p.m.; Sat, 12 to 11 p.m.; Sun, 12 to 8 p.m.

L eave Your Mark." That's the Three Notch'd Brewing motto.

Sounds simple enough, but it's not always easy to do when you are a brewery opening up at the same time as lots of others breweries in the same region. You have to have a plan for how to differentiate yourself from the pack.

Three Notch'd Brewing is doing it. They're leaving their mark with their successful beers like the **Hydraulion Red**, a red Irish-style ale with both a caramel and citrusy profile, which helped them achieve national recognition when they won a Bronze Medal at the 2014 Great American Beer Festival.

40-Mile IPA
Style: India Pale Ale
ABV: 5.7%
Availability: Year-round

You're first drawn to the aromas of fruitiness—tangerine, citrus, and tropical smells. Those who scope out some great West Coast–style IPAs will enjoy the 40-Mile IPA brewed in this style, with a refined bitterness flavor that you get from all the American hops paired with a light malt body. This beer is named "after the number of miles raced to warn Thomas Jefferson and his state legislators that Cornwallis had ordered their capture" during the Revolutionary War.

They're leaving their mark on the Charlottesville community, by partnering with local businesses, which they're doing for some of their beer recipes, an example being the **"Jack's Java" Espresso Stout**, a rich oatmeal stout that uses a "special three roast coffee blend" from the Shenandoah Coffee roasters directly across the street from the brewery.

The Three Notch'd team is also working on doing more collaborations with other craft breweries, particularly ones that they highly respect, breweries that have already left their mark on the craft beer industry around the US. One of those is Oskar Blues Brewery, a brewery they were able to partner with in recent months. The result of that is a black ale released in January 2015 called **"Black and Goldings,"** so named for the city of Pittsburgh, where Dave Warwick, brewmaster at Three Notch'd and Tim Matthews, brewmaster at Oskar Blues, first met while assistant brewers in two crosstown brewpubs.

Together Dave and the founders Scott, George, and Derek develop their beer names with their motto in mind too; many of the beers are named for memorable people who have left their mark in history. That includes **The Ghost American Pale Ale**, a pale ale "with an ambush of dry hops," named for John Singleton Mosby, one of the heroic cavalry officers of the Confederate army during the Civil War.

Their beer is all made in a building filled with its own meaningful history—one of the individually protected buildings in the city of Charlottesville. Constructed in 1937, it was part of the headquarters building of Monticello Dairy for decades, a production factory for ice cream, butter, milk, and other dairy products. Today it's been repurposed as a production factory for beer. The beer is made in the back rooms of their property, a great setup that includes a 20-barrel brew system, 3-barrel pilot system, and 400 barrels of fermentation space, while the front is dedicated to a roomy tasting room.

The tasting room incorporates an attractive combination of new and old things. A padded bench extends the length of the front wall and there is a set of red leather contemporary-style chairs. There's a room to the right of the entrance with board games and more tables. A brick-designed bar area, lamp fixtures along the front wall, and the original windows all retain some of that old colonial feel.

DEVILS BACKBONE BASECAMP BREWPUB *phenomanol food 3/27/16*
great Beer!

200 Mosbys Run, Roseland, VA 22967; (434) 361-1001; dbbrewingcompany.com;
@dbbrewingco

Founded: 1998 **Founder:** Steven and Heidi Crandall **Brewers:** Jason Oliver, Aaron Reilly
Flagship Beer: Vienna Lager **Year-Round Beers:** Gold Leaf Lager, Eight Point IPA,
Striped Bass Pale Ale, Vienna Lager, Schwartz Bier, Trail Angel Weiss **Seasonals/Special
Releases:** Old Virginia Gold, Reilly's Red, Low Hanging Fruit, Rute Bier, Turbo Cougar (see
website for full list)

Upon entering the Devils Backbone Basecamp Brewpub, the taxidermy display
throughout the brewpub was the first thing I was personally drawn to, because
it made me immediately reminisce about my grandfather's hunting cabin (a cabin
that we all still regularly visit), where the main living area is filled with taxidermy
such as a black bear, an 11-point buck head, and a few other stuffed deer. The Devils
Backbone Basecamp Brewpub takes the taxidermy decorations to an entirely new
level!

Central Virginia

You're greeted by a big black bear, looming over the host desk in the center of the entrance. Next to the black bear you'll see two other black bears that look like they're climbing up the wall next to you.

At the long bar, enjoy the experience of an afternoon or evening inside this impressive mountain ski lodge brewpub while you gaze at the other taxidermy; you'll see coyote, deer, turkeys, goats, and rams, among other things. A few of the animals showcased in the Basecamp Brewpub's interior are personal possessions of co-founder Steven Crandall—ones he hunted and shot himself.

The brewpub's interior has its own wow factor, but it's about to become an even more incredible destination outside in the coming months. It already has the view of a lifetime from its position next to the striking Blue Ridge Mountains, based on 100 acres of land. It will soon offer more opportunities to relish in this view with the addition of Basecamp Brewpub & Meadows, a planned 5-acre bier garden that will include food stations, an outdoor bar, and as co-founder Heidi Crandall shares, "secret gardens"—little nooks of private tables where you can feel like you're having your own private party, even though in actuality you'll be surrounded by hundreds, or possibly thousands, of other customers.

Last but not least, you can enjoy this experience at the Basecamp Brewpub knowing that you'll have plenty of amazing beer, beer that has helped Devils

Backbone win the Mid-Sized Brewing Company and Mid-Sized Brew Team of the Year at the 2014 Great American Beer Festival. Since they've opened, they've received close to 25 various Great American Beer Festival awards for a number of their beers, among countless other awards at the World Beer Cup and other competitions. Start with their flagship, the **Vienna Lager**, a malty and slightly sweet crisp lager made from a multi-stage mash. Move on to the equally crisp and balanced **Schwartz Bier** that has taken home its share of awards in recent years. On beautiful days sitting outside at the new bier garden, try the light, golden-colored **Gold Leaf Lager** or the **Trail Angel Weiss**, a Bavarian-style hefeweizen that is an ideal drink for a bier garden setting.

Originally producing its beer on an 8-barrel German brew system at the brewpub, Devils Backbone now also has an outpost production facility in Lexington, Virginia, to help meet the demands for all this stand-out beer (see Shenandoah Valley chapter). This is a whole other road trip you'll want to experience—as a separate adventure on a different day.

That's because near to the Basecamp Brewpub, one of the many breweries located on the Brew Ridge Trail (see Beer Bus Tours & Self-Guided Trails chapter), there are plenty of other breweries to see, including Blue Mountain Brewery, Wild Wolf Brewing, and Starr Hill Brewery. If you don't want to drive, you can hop on a bus tour.

Whatever you do, don't leave without taking advantage of this outdoor mecca, using the Basecamp Brewpub as your reward after a full day of hiking or cycling throughout the region.

SOUTH STREET BREWERY *Great food huge flight glasses*
106 South St. West, Charlottesville, VA 22902; (434) 293-6550; southstreetbrewery
.com; @SouthStBrewery
Founded: 1998 **Founders:** Fred Greenewalt, Duffy Pappas (business purchased by Mandi and Taylor Smack in 2014) **Brewers:** Taylor Smack, Mitch Hamilton **Flagship Beer:** Satan's Pony **Beers:** Virginia Ale, My Personal Helles, 365 Shandy, Barhopper, Absolution, Hogwaller Kölsch, J.P. Ale, Slippery When Wit, Bumper Crop, Deep Friar, Anastasia's Chocolate Fantasy (see website for all specifics including availability of beers)

Situated at a prime spot in downtown Charlottesville, South Street Brewery is a well-known Charlottesville landmark to the town's residents, having existed since 1998. The building itself is a recognizable landmark in the town's history, having existed since 1899.

So when the original founders of South Street Brewery made the decision to sell, Mandi and Taylor Smack, owners of the Blue Mountain Brewery and Blue Mountain

Barrel House, knew they wanted to preserve the legacy of South Street Brewery, while also giving it new life.

One of their ways of doing that was to renovate the interior and open up the many closed-in spaces. The old copper bar top was replaced, and the original copper was re-used as a kind of modern art display throughout the brewpub's interior. The building's stunning old character remains, from the exposed beams to the brick fireplace as the centerpiece of the room. If you're lucky you might be able to secure a seat on one of the couches in front of that fireplace while you enjoy one of their 12 different kinds of beer.

The beer is also a mixture of old and new traditions. There's the flagship, the **Satan's Pony**, a medium-bodied amber ale. Or the **Absolution**, an old mild ale with a malty richness, a nice choice when you're able to snag one of those seats by the fire. On warmer days, grab a seat at one of the tables next to the large, looming windows in front and try a concoction like the **365 Shandy**, a blend of a light crisp beer mixed with lemonade.

Enjoy the diverse array of pub food, and the wonderful smells that will draw you

in from the moment you enter the front door of the brewpub. There's hearty food like burgers, steaks, and pork. Choose from charcuterie boards and cheese plates. There's a selection of salads for a lighter fare option—though you'll have trouble ordering the healthy choice when you have options that pair nicely with your craft beer, like the mac 'n' cheese—especially when you know you can make your own mac 'n' cheese creation, adding ingredients such as pulled chicken, lump crab meat, or applewood smoked bacon.

WATERSTONE PIZZA (JEFFERSON STREET BREWERY)

1309 Jefferson St., Lynchburg, VA 24504; (434) 455-1515; jeffersonstreetbrewery .com

Founded: 2008 **Founder:** Scott Young **Brewer:** Wesley Chastain **Year-Round Beers:** Honey Wheat, American Pale Ale, Oatmeal Stout, Light, Amber Ale **Seasonals/Special Releases:** N/A

You will get more than a tasty wood-fired pizza and a microbrewed beer during your visit to Waterstone; you'll also get a taste of history as you drive through the Bluffwalk Center, where Waterstone is located, which includes not only Waterstone but also the Craddock-Terry Hotel and an event center. As it states

on Waterstone's website, "all three distinct entities were built inside the historic Craddock-Terry Shoe Factory and William King Jr. tobacco warehouse buildings." The Craddock-Terry Shoe Factory was a huge part of Lynchburg's history, and the largest employer in Lynchburg for many years. The company was once the largest shoemaker in the South, and it existed for almost 100 years, from 1889 until the mid 1980s.

What does all this have to do with beer? Well, not much, but the truth is you can't visit here without soaking in all this amazing history throughout this area of Lynchburg. While you reflect on it, enjoy one of the 5 signature beers including the popular **Honey Wheat**, a golden beer brewed with coriander and orange peel. Or try the **American Pale Ale**, where you'll be able to taste the delicious caramel malt while also experiencing the bitterness throughout and in the finish as a result of the Columbus hops. The **Oatmeal Stout** will please those who prefer a maltier beer, full bodied with a creamy texture.

WILD WOLF BREWING COMPANY

2461 Rockfish Valley Hwy., Nellysford, VA 22958; (434) 361-0088; wildwolfbeer .com; @WildWolfBeer
Founded: 2011 Founders: Mary Wolf, Danny Wolf **Brewer:** Danny Wolf **Flagship Beers:** Blonde Hunny **Year-Round Beers:** American Pilsner, Blonde Hunny, Alpha Ale, Wee Heavy, Dry Stout, Primal Instinct IPA **Seasonal/Specialty Beers:**, Strawberry Schwarzcake, Exquisitely Evil Ale, WolfNStein, Anniversary Ale, Kick IT

In Virginia's Nelson County, Route 151 is a spectacular, scenic drive along the foothills of the Blue Ridge Mountains. Beyond the drive alone, it's also become a travel and tourist destination, and above all, a haven for wine and craft beer lovers.

Mary and Danny Wolf, mother and son team and co-founders of Wild Wolf Brewing, hunted these roads often on their search for the spot to set up their brewpub and restaurant business. They knew they wanted to be on Route 151, particularly along what's also now known as the Brew Ridge Trail (brewridgetrail.com), a marketed self-guided trail that provides maps, a sample itinerary, and information about touring the breweries.

When they found the land they desired for their business, they also found a 100-plus-year-old schoolhouse along with it, a unique property full of character (though with plenty of quirks as Mary has now learned firsthand). That schoolhouse now functions as a restaurant and dining experience that Mary describes as "farm-to-fork," which is quite appropriate when you understand a little more about their daily restaurant operations; bread is made in house and most of their meats come in as whole animals, where they are butchered, brined, and smoked onsite. Eggs

from the chickens that roam outside in the hop yard are used in the kitchen.

Their philosophy carries over to the beer; the hops they grow outside are used in their beer, as in the **Primal Instinct IPA**, an American IPA that blends five different kinds of malts and five different kinds of hops together. Consider trying the **Exquisitely Evil Ale**, a hoppy golden-colored ale that uses over 55 pounds of hops in its batch recipe. Get a sample tray of their 5 house beers or their seasonal beers while you sit in the old schoolhouse/restaurant.

Or, choose to sit at the bar in back, a new building that they added on to the schoolhouse. It connects via a hallway and now houses the bar and the brewery, a 15-barrel brewing system. Outside you may soon need a map to find your way

around; it's turned into a whole complex of buildings and structures as Wild Wolf has grown, including an enclosed outdoor pavilion where there's live music on the weekends, an outdoor beer garden in front that's ideal for those customers who want to bring along their dog, a small house that functions as the gift shop, and a recently added event hall that is used for private events like weddings and big parties.

This mother and son family operation works very effectively. Danny is the brewmaster, who Mary describes as a "versatile brewer who doesn't always follow the style guides . . . (he brews) unique beers that people love." One of those is their flagship beer, the Blonde Hunny, a Belgian-style blonde ale that uses heaps of honey instead of sugar.

Mary's background is in product marketing and she talks passionately about how exciting it is to "see a product come to life and use skills and strengths from the past." At one point she decided to take an early retirement. That was prior to Danny graduating from brewing school, prior to what has now become more than a full-time job. But she's happy. Mary has played a major role in creating a successful business that just keeps on growing. Needless to say, retirement is no longer part of her vocabulary these days.

Beer Bars

BEER RUN

**156 Carlton Rd., Suite 203, Charlottesville, VA 22902; (434) 984-2337; beerrun
.com; @BeerRunVA**
Draft Beers: 17 **Bottled/Canned Beers:** Call or see website for specifics (website
specifies an A–Z list of breweries that they usually stock or have readily available)

Beer Run is definitely a craft beer bar, but it's also definitely a bottle shop. It also could be defined as a wine shop and a wine bar. Some customers may claim it's a restaurant. Everyone would be right.

There are multiple reasons to visit this place, but the beer selection is the big draw, so sit at the bar, order one of the rotating draft selections or order from the long list of bottles, and then shop for your take-out beer on the shelves behind you or at the packed-full bottle shop that's adjacent to your barstool. As if you needed another reason, it also made *Draft* magazine's 2014 list for 100 Best American Beer Bars.

Charlottesville—Pub Crawl

The four stops on this pub crawl allow you to tour four unique beer establishments as well as get a feel for the historic downtown Charlottesville area. The total walking distance over the course of the day will be approximately 1.5 miles—a great way to get a little exercise and make you thirsty for that next beer sampling.

Three Notch'd Brewing, 946 Grady Ave., Charlottesville, VA 22903; (434) 293-0610; threenotchdbrewing.com. Three Notch'd Brewing is based in the old Monticello dairy building in Charlottesville and it's a great spot to start to see some of the old preserved colonial features while also relaxing in a beautifully laid out tasting room. Choose from sampler flights of 4 or 6 beers, and if you want a snack there's salsa and chips for sale at the bar, or there's usually a food cart stationed right outside the door.

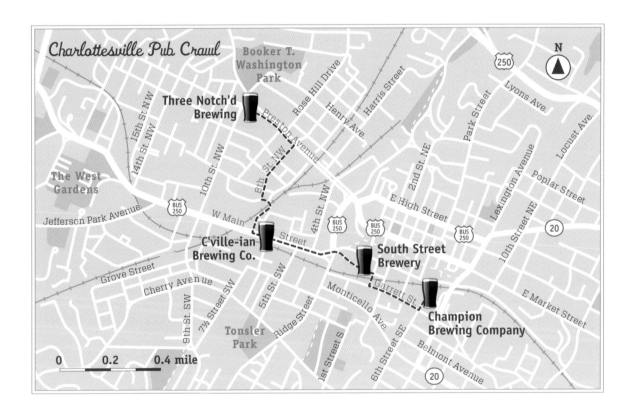

Take a right as you leave Three Notch'd (passing McGrady's Irish Pub), then continue onto Preston Avenue. Turn right onto 8th Street NW. Follow that for .25 mile, then take a slight left onto 8th Lane N, a right onto 8th Street NW, then a left onto Main Street. C'ville-ian Brewing will be on your left.

C'ville-ian Brewing Co., 705 W. Main St., Charlottesville, VA 22903; (434) 328-2252; cvillebrewco.com. A new addition to the downtown Charlottesville beer scene, this small nanobrewery has a laid-back tasting room and a small brewhouse in back. Get a flight while you check out the mini US flags that decorate the tasting room as well as read the beer quotes on the wall from historical figures like Benjamin Franklin and Abraham Lincoln. No food here, only beer, but that's okay, as your next stop on the pub crawl is South Street Brewery and you should build up an appetite for this place.

Head east (take a left) out of C'ville-ian and walk about a quarter of a mile or so and continue onto South Street West until you see South Street Brewery on your right (total distance is less than a half mile).

South Street Brewery, 106 South St. West, Charlottesville, VA 22902; (434) 293-6550; southstreetbrewery.com. A landmark brewpub in downtown Charlottesville since the late '90s, South Street Brewery is usually a great beer stop for residents of the Charlottesville area. The owners of Blue Mountain Brewery and Barrel House purchased it in 2014, and today it is still a great beer and food stop. If you're hungry by now, you'll get your chance to eat, with a brewpub menu that has everything from steaks to burgers to fresh salads to mac 'n' cheese.

Take a right when you leave South Street Brewery, then another immediate right onto 1st Street South. Cross over the railroad tracks, then take a left onto Garrett. Follow Garrett Street until you get to 6th Street SE, take a left onto 6th Street SE, and you will see Champion Brewing on your right.

Champion Brewing Company, 324 6th St. SE, Charlottesville, VA 22902; (434) 295-2739; championbrewingcompany.com. End your pub crawl by settling in for a sampling tray or a beer at Champion Brewing's tasting room, that's industrial looking but also warm, with a great American beer bar feel where you can watch sports inside or enjoy seating outside on the patio.

Central Virginia

Shenandoah Valley

On your excursions throughout the Shenandoah Valley region, take in the views of the scenic mountain ranges that surround you after a day of hiking the Blue Ridge or Allegheny Mountains or exploring sights like battlefields, caverns, or the birthplace of Woodrow Wilson.

If you're there on vacation, make sure you allot plenty of time on your stopover to explore the 10+ breweries that are now based in this region. These breweries are each distinctive, ranging from nanobreweries based on cow and herb farms to large 20,000-square-foot facilities such as Devils Backbone Outpost Brewery in Lexington—a quickly expanding craft brewery currently in the process of constructing new brewing equipment systems that will increase their future capacity to 250,000 barrels of beer per year.

Many of these breweries also offer easy access on and off I-81, a route that starts at the US/Canada border just south of Ontario and continues all the way south to Dandridge, Tennessee—a viable option for your next beer road trip.

Breweries

BACKROOM BREWERY

150 Ridgemont Rd., Middletown, VA 22645; (540) 869-8482; backroombreweryva
.com; @BackroomBrews
Founded: 2013 **Founder:** Billie Clifton **Brewer:** Andy Cummings **Flagship Beer:** N/A
Year-Round Beers: Backroom Blonde, Rosemary Orange Amber Ale, Helltown Red IPA,
Lemon Basil, Kiss Me Kolsch, Reliance Road Red (see website for specifics) **Seasonals/
Special Releases:** Cilantro Lime, Black Truffle Pig Black IPA, Chile Pepper Red Ale, Hop
Harvest Party Ale **Tours:** No **Taproom:** Wed to Sun, 10 a.m. to 8 p.m.

Escape from the I-81 truck traffic into the Virginia countryside, where just a
short 3 miles from exit 302 you'll come across a peaceful oasis in the form of an
herb farm and flower garden called Sunflower Cottage. See and smell the fresh herbs
first in the greenhouses and gardens, then enjoy the taste of those herbs inside your
beer. In addition to the herbs like the bittering hops—some of which are grown
directly on their farm in a hop field—you'll also get to taste beer recipes accentu-
ated with herbs like cilantro, basil, and rosemary.

Try the **Rosemary Orange Amber**, a tasty ale that serves as a nice refreshment when the sun's out and you can sit outside in Backroom Brewery's beer garden and patio. Sample flavorful herb-enhanced beer like the **Cilantro Lime**, a "wheat beer . . . with cilantro picked directly from the greenhouses." Seasonal beers like the **Chile Pepper Red Ale** use habaneros straight from the farm. For a more traditional beer, there are also options such as the **Reliance Road Red**, an Irish-style red ale at 6% ABV.

Mark your calendar for some of their annual events, particularly the Hop Harvest Party every August, where local residents come to Sunflower Cottage and help to pick the hops from the vines and enjoy a free dinner afterward. Minutes after the hops are picked, many of them are thrown directly into the kettle to be used in their batch of Hop Harvest Party Ale. Billie Clifton, founder of Backroom Brewery, informs me that they planted their hop field back in 2012. The hops came before the brewery.

The brewery started small with 5-gallon batches. Today there's a 3.5-barrel system with 7-barrel fermenters. Inside the brewery tasting room it's cozy, with a country store look and feel; only this country store also includes a bar and a full kitchen, with made-from-scratch food. As in their beer menu, their food selections make use of the many fresh produce and herb options grown onsite, with a menu complete with options like a Beer Bread Grilled Cheese, beef sliders with basil mayo, and a chicken salad sandwich made with farm-grown tarragon and grapes.

Lemon Basil
Style: Wheat Ale
ABV: 4.75%
Availability: Year-round on tap and in bottles
available at the tasting room

Your senses will perk up when you smell the aromas of the beer, with scents of lemon, pepper, and mint. Wheat ale is a great base for this beer, a particularly nice malt base for the lemon and basil flavors. It's an incredibly refreshing beer and non–beer drinkers should be pleasantly surprised by its refreshing, citrusy, and spicy attributes.

An outdoor patio with tables and games like cornhole enables customers to sit outside on a sunny day and enjoy the countryside around them. Backroom Brewery is both kid friendly and pet friendly—where you can enjoy craft beer and food in a relaxing country atmosphere.

BIG LICK BREWING COMPANY

135 Salem Ave. SW #100, Roanoke, VA 24011; (540) 562-8383; biglickbrewingco
.com; @biglickbrewing
Founded: 2014 **Founders:** Bryan Summerson, Chuck Garot **Brewer:** Bryan Summerson
Flagship Beer: Peace, Love and Hoppiness Double IPA **Year-Round Beers:** N/A, all
beers are small batch releases **Seasonals/Special Releases:** Nippy Lil' Bugger Spiced
Amber Ale, Strange Magik, Status Quo Cream Ale, Burn Out Bright Saison **Tours:** No
Taproom: Thurs and Fri, 4 to 9 p.m.; Sat, 1 to 9 p.m.

After many consecutive years of purchasing bigger and better brew equipment for his homebrewing hobby, co-founder Bryan Summerson's wife encouraged him, "You need to start making money instead of spending it." With the help of co-founder Chuck Garot and other valuable friendships—like his cousin, who owns the building where Big Lick Brewing Company is now based—he set off to build a business.

It's amazing what Bryan and Chuck were able to pack in to approximately 1,500 square feet of space: a 2-barrel brew system, a small room to store all the fermenters, and a cozy tasting room area with a bar and a few tables for customer seating. Historical memorabilia completes the interior design of the tasting room, much of it a representation of Roanoke's past.

Some of that interior design comes in the form of ceiling and floor joints from the historic Roanoke Woolworth building that were just taking up room in storage, and are now repurposed as part of the tasting room design. The foot rails at the bar were also going to waste, found buried in the concrete at the back of the building. Co-founder Chuck built the light fixtures hanging above the bar out of old Roanoke Railhouse growlers. On the walls, you can find other framed representations of the past: tickets and coupons—food vouchers that Roanoke residents were provided with during the Depression, old Roanoke newspaper clippings, and a picture of Chuck's dad climbing up the Roanoke Star the night before it became a Roanoke landmark. Erected in 1949, that 100-foot-tall star is now a symbol for Roanoke, "The Star City of the South," visible from around the city.

Both co-founders still work full-time jobs, and in their hours outside of work can regularly be found at the brewery, brewing the beer and serving the customers. Because of their system size, they don't necessarily have any year-round beers. They strive to constantly create new recipes, and in the first 7-month period that they were open they managed to crank out 35 different beers. Rave reviews were received for the **Nippy Lil' Bugger**, a spiced winter amber ale with full-flavored malts and the **Strange Magik**, a complex peanut butter porter. They constantly experiment with different types of IPAs, and now have an ongoing IPA series (so far 4 different kinds—by the time you read this there'll probably be 10!).

Free popcorn in the tasting room is always available from a machine in the corner, and food trucks are frequently stationed outside on the weekends. Big Lick's location in downtown Roanoke is convenient to some new downtown apartment complexes and renovated warehouses that have turned into lofts, an easy walk for residents to enjoy a beer or purchase a growler to go.

Beer Lover's Pick

Time the Avenger
Style: IPA
ABV: 4.7%
Availability: Special release

Big Lick's Session IPA beer refers to the fact that "time is the worst enemy to a hop-forward beer." Point: Drink it immediately. You'll want to when you taste the full-bodied elements and flavors that you'd expect to get from a higher-alcohol IPA in a beer that's only 4.7% ABV. Lots of hops in the aroma and taste, but the combination of US and British base malts create a great balance.

BLUE LAB BREWING COMPANY

123 S. Randolph St., Lexington, VA 24450; (540) 458-0146; bluelabbrewing.com;
@bluelabbrewing

Founded: 2010 **Founders:** Bill Hamilton, Tom Lovell **Brewer:** Bill Hamilton **Flagship Beer:** India Pale Ale, Irish Red Ale **Year-Round Beers:** American Stout, Irish Red Ale, India Pale Ale, Pale Ale, **Seasonals/Special Releases:** Hefeweizen, Green Chile Ale, Imperial IPA, Oktoberfest, Christmas Ale, Fresh Hop Ale **Tours:** Upon request/if staff has availability **Taproom:** Wed and Thurs, 4:30 to 8 p.m.; Fri, 4:30 to 9 p.m.; Sat, 2 to 9 p.m.

While attending college at Washington and Lee University in Lexington, a group of friends purchased a 20-gallon brew system. This was the beginning of Bill Hamilton and Tom Lovell's journey into brewing; they were two members of that original group who decided to take the college beer brewing a step further many years later after they each pursued careers outside of the brewing industry (careers they still are working full-time).

They knew that the historic downtown Lexington area was the place they wanted to open their brewery, and opportunity came in the form of an approximately 1,800-square-foot old doctor's office building.

Rooms that once served as individual patient rooms within that doctor's office now house the equipment; they started with a 1-barrel system, advanced to a bigger 2-barrel system, then graduated to an even bigger 5- to 6-barrel quantity that they're now producing with every batch.

Irish Red Ale
Style: Irish Ale
ABV: 4.5%
Availability: Year-round on tap

An overall smooth and balanced beer, this Irish ale has a beautiful deep red color, a well-defined malt base with some toasted flavors, some subtle British hops to add a touch of bitterness, and a dry finish.

All of this beer is made primarily for Blue Lab Brewery's tasting room, a small, intimate space that occasionally offers trivia nights, live music, and above all a great atmosphere to enjoy a beer with your friends. Bill and Tom describe it as a "neighborhood corner pub."

This neighborhood pub puts out the kind of interesting beer selection that you may or may not always expect to see at your regular neighborhood spot. **Green Chile Ale** is available in the summer months, made by adding roasted New Mexico green chiles to the brew tank. You can also get more popular lighter styles like the **Hefeweizen** or **Belgian Wit**, hoppier varieties like an **Imperial IPA**, or dark, malty beers like a **Baltic Porter** with some delicious notes of caramel and molasses.

BROTHERS CRAFT BREWING
800 N. Main St., Harrisonburg, VA 22802; (540) 421-6599; brotherscraftbrewing.com; @broscraftbrew
Founded: 2012 **Founders:** Adam, Jason, and Tyler Shifflett **Brewers:** Adam and Tyler Shifflett **Flagship Beer:** Hoptimization, Great Outdoors Virginia Pale Ale, The Admiral Double IPA **Year-Round Beers:** Same as flagships **Seasonals/Special Releases:** Fairgrounds Fall Ale, Daylight Cravings, Resolute, Rum Barrel Aged Belgian Dubbel, Good Adweiss **Tours:** No **Taproom:** Mon, 6 to 10 p.m.; Thurs, 4 to 11 p.m.; Fri, 4 to 11 p.m., Sat, 12 to 11 p.m.; Sun, 12:30 to 8 p.m.

Brothers Craft Brewing (originally Three Brothers Brewing) was founded by—you guessed it—three brothers: Adam, Jason, and Tyler Shifflett. Their brewery's location in downtown Harrisonburg is important because it is in the region where

Resolute Bourbon Barrel Imperial Stout
Style: Imperial Stout
ABV: 13.5%
Availability: Limited release in 750ml bottles

There's no denying the complex full flavors emerging from this strong stout. In demand among beer geeks everywhere, it's aged in bourbon barrels for 9 months. Its dark chocolate bitterness and rich malty base comes through in every sip. It's one to savor and sip, and enjoy slowly—as you will clearly taste the intense, evolving sweetness throughout the initial taste and finish due to its whopping 13.5% ABV.

they were born and raised. Their location choice also proved to be ideal for their needs, an old Coca-Cola bottling plant that has both historic significance to the town and a great infrastructure already in place for their new brewery.

Within that building, they have constructed a spacious industrial-looking tasting room, where through glass, you can look into the brewhouse and admire the nice-sized 15-barrel brew system and 30- and 60-barrel fermenters where all the magic happens.

In addition to the spacious tasting room, there is a private room that's available to rent out for special events. There's live music and food trucks at least three nights a week, and more importantly usually 8 beers on tap. Try one of their flagships like **The Great Outdoors**, a crisp well-balanced Virginia pale ale, or opt for something that will pack in a more bitter punch, like the **Admiral Double IPA**. In addition to all the usual suspects and beer styles, Brothers Craft Brewing also has some barrel-aged beers, and a nice selection of their products is available to purchase in cans, 12-ounce bottles, and some occasional 750ml bottle varieties.

CHAOS MOUNTAIN BREWING

3135 Dillons Mill Rd., Callaway, VA 24067; (540) 334-1600; chaosmountainbrewing .com; @ChaosMtnBrewing
Founded: 2014 **Founders:** Joe and Wendy Hallock **Brewer:** Will Landry **Flagship Beers:** Mad Hopper IPA, Squatch Ale Scotch Ale **Year-Round Beers:** Mad Hopper IPA, Squatch Ale Scotch Ale, Agents of Chaos Belgian Special Dark, 4 Mad Chefs Quadrupel, Cheeky Monkey Belgian Blonde **Seasonals/Special Releases:** Cocoborealis Triple Chocolate Stout, Edge of the Sun Lime Lager, The Legless Horseman Pumpkin Ale (see website for specifics) **Tours:** For private groups and upon request **Taproom:** Thurs and Fri, 4 to 9 p.m.; Sat, 1 to 9 p.m.; Sun, 12 to 6 p.m.

If it wouldn't have been for an empty 20,000-square-foot building at the base of Cahas Mountain, the plan for Chaos Mountain Brewery may never have been devised. Once used as a manufacturing facility for co-founder Joe Hallock's previous business—making beds for people with special needs—this massive building was no longer in use. When he and his wife, Wendy, sold their interest in that business, this building south of Roanoke was theirs. Joe envisioned it would make a great brewery.

Fortunately he didn't just envision it. He put his vision into action and built it.

Through homebrewing meet-ups, Joe and Wendy met their head brewer, Will Landry, a homebrewer himself who also went to brewing school and was passionate about getting into the brewery business full-time. This team is now running a serious brewing operation.

With a 30-barrel system and a 7-barrel pilot system, they are distributing their beers from Richmond and other areas south and west of Richmond throughout the state, as well as serving up an average of 12 to 14 beers on tap at their tasting room. There's something for everyone with this beer selection. Belgian-style beers like the

Mad Hopper IPA
Style: India Pale Ale
ABV: 6.7%
Availability: Year-round on tap and sold in
    12-ounce sixpacks
A nice golden color and an addition of citrus and resiny hops complete this delicious IPA. It has a great medium- to full-bodied flavor without overpowering bitterness.

Cheeky Monkey, a Belgian blonde ale, and the **Agents of Chaos**, a Belgian special dark beer, are part of the lineup, as well as beers like the **Squatch Ale**, a malty Scottish ale. They've recently started to produce the **Cross Czech Pilsner** to serve to their tasting room customers for a lighter, golden lager experience as the craft equivalent of some of the mainstream beer brands that customers might be used to drinking.

Visit the tasting room during the Thursday through Sunday open hours where you'll generally find live music and food trucks, as well as a wide-open space where you can admire the brew tanks behind the bar and take in the fresh mountain air outside. From Roanoke, it's about a 35-minute, often winding drive on country roads, and that's what makes it fun. It's a destination worth checking out on your next beer trip.

DEVILS BACKBONE OUTPOST BREWERY
50 Northwind Ln., Lexington, VA 24450; (540) 462-6200; dbbrewingcompany.com; @dbbrewingco
Founded: 2008 (Devils Backbone Company founded 2008, Outpost Brewery built in 2011)
Founders: Steven and Heidi Crandall **Brewers:** Jason Oliver, Nate Olewine **Flagship Beers:** Vienna Lager, Schwartz Bier, Eight Point IPA **Year-Round Beers:** Gold Leaf Lager, Striped Bass, Vienna Lager, Schwartz Bier, Eight Point IPA **Seasonals/Special Releases:** Pumpkin Hunter, Kilt Flasher, Bravo Four Point Session IPA **Tours:** Sat and Sun, 2, 3, 4 and 5 p.m. **Taproom:** Sun and Mon, 1 to 7 p.m.; Tues and Wed, 1 to 8 p.m.; Thurs to Sat, 1 to 9 p.m.

The Devils Backbone motto is "Craft an Adventure." Founders Steve and Heidi Crandall's own journey in the brewing business thus far has been its own adventure. During a private tour of the brewery with Heidi, she described just how much the business has transformed and expanded since the start. Her excitement in sharing their story is evident, and her passion for the business is just as evident. Every day is a new adventure.

It all started with a 100-acre property that the Crandalls owned in Nelson County. Their background in the custom building business prepared them for what came next—an idea to build a brewpub—Devils Backbone Basecamp Brewpub—from the ground up. Surrounded by the Blue Ridge Mountains with a rustic, ski-lodge atmosphere inside, it is both an experience as well as a destination. (See Devils Backbone Basecamp Brewpub in the Central Virginia chapter.)

When demand surpassed supply in a very short time period based on what their 8-barrel brewhouse at the Basecamp was producing, the Outpost production facility and taproom was built (also from the ground up) in Lexington, an attractive, rural location in a quaint town that's also close to a major thoroughfare (I-81).

In the short 3-year period since they opened the Outpost in 2011, they expanded a number of times. But they knew they would need to expand again, so they decided to take the plunge and go big. Really big. Engineers are building a 120-barrel Rolec brewhouse and much of that construction and engineering is taking place onsite, one part at a time. During my visit there was a nonstop flurry of activity everywhere I looked, a full-fledged 24/7 operation. Brewers carry out responsibilities over three separate shifts, allowing round the clock beer-making on their current 30-barrel system until the new brewhouse is officially operational. There's a control room as well as a lab built specifically for use by the quality assurance director. Any beer geek would be in heaven surrounded by all these brew tanks and efficient, automated systems. It takes beer-making to a whole new level.

By the time you read this book, it is highly likely that Devils Backbone will have a capacity of 250,000 barrels a year. Need help visualizing just how much beer this is? Approximately 63 million US pints!

Quite a few of those barrels will be filled up with their flagship beers, like the **Schwartz Bier**, a German-style malty black lager that's dark black in color. Beer is distributed in bottles and cans and there are highly automated bottling and canning lines at the Outpost facility. They have a can series of beers, which includes beer such as the **Gold Leaf Lager**, a golden-colored pilsner that is already a four-time Great American Beer Festival winner. In the spring and summer months, try a can of the **Rail Angel Weiss**, a Bavarian-style weissbier.

Beer Lover's Pick

Vienna Lager
Style: Lager
ABV: 4.9%
Availability: Year-round on tap and in bottles
Vienna-style lagers are known for their low hop presence, malt sweetness, and a crisp mouth feel. The Devils Backbone brewing team masters this style with their subtle use of noble hops and layered toasted malt flavor.

While you sip on the weissbier, you can sit outside at picnic-style tables and enjoy the countryside views of Lexington. A tasting room inside, open 7 days a week, is a nice hideout for the colder months, where you can buy sampler flights, fill up growlers, purchase memorabilia, or pick up to-go packs of bottles or cans. Tours of the brewery are Saturday and Sunday every hour from 2 to 5 p.m. throughout the afternoon.

The Devils Backbone team's efforts haven't gone unnoticed. That brew team, including brewmaster Jason Oliver and lead brewer Nate Olewine, works hard to make a strong range of products that customers love. At the Great American Beer Festival, it has paid off. They've won multiple awards. In 2012 they were named Small Brewpub and Small Brewpub Brewer of the Year. In 2013 they won Small Brewing Company and Small Brewing Company Brewer. In 2014 they won Mid-Sized Brewing Company and Brew Team of the Year.

At this pace of growth, they won't be in the mid-sized category for much longer.

FLYING MOUSE BREWERY
221 Precast Way, Troutville, VA 24175; (540) 992-1288; flyingmousebrewery.com; @flyingmousebrew
Founded: 2013 **Founders:** Frank Moeller (Debbie Moeller, Chris Moeller, John Garrett, Jim Trexel—Leadership/Directors) **Brewer:** Frank Moeller **Flagship Beers:** Flying Mouse Three-Kölsch, Flying Mouse Five—Pale Ale, Flying Mouse Eight—Porter **Year-Round Beers:** Same as flagships and Flying Mouse Four—Smooth Hop IPA **Seasonals/Special Releases:** Aztec Chocolate, Fruitcake Amber, Brown Ale, Summer Wheat **Tours:** Upon request **Taproom:** Fri, 4 to 8 p.m.; Sat, 2 to 8 p.m.; Sun, 1 to 5 p.m.

Ask the Flying Mouse team to share the story of Bartleby Hopsworth, their official mascot, the mouse who dreamed of flight, or read the Bartleby story on their website, to better understand how the name of the brewery aligns with their philosophy. Bartleby was an adventurer, like many of those who cycle on the Bicentennial TransAmerica Bike Trail (that crosses paths with the brewery), or the hikers who travel the Appalachian Trail, located a half-mile away. The Flying Mouse team makes it one of their goals to "promote and support outdoor activity as part of a healthy lifestyle," Frank Moeller, founder and brewer, shares.

It's an ideal spot to stop for a break after a long cycling or hiking workout, and the brewery and taproom is designed as an "indoor/outdoor experience." When you're having a beer in the taproom, you feel like you're in the center of the action as you admire the tanks around you, and as a result you have an opportunity to learn and discover as much as you want to know about how the beer is made.

The **Flying Mouse Eight**, a smoky, full-flavored beer, is the kind of beer you can expect during your visit and is also packaged in cans (they voted in favor of packaging in cans vs. bottles to stick with their objective to promote outdoor activities). At the tasting room, you might also see one or two of their seasonal varieties, like the **Aztec Chocolate**, made with Chilean dark chocolate malt and brewed with cayenne peppers, or the **Fruitcake Amber** that uses dried fruits in the recipe.

Frank, like many in the business, started the brewery out of the desire to turn his hobby into a business, and his 20+ years in homebrewing, background in mechanical engineering, and passion for cooking all seemed to be a great base in order to create this brewery in Troutville that has been opening their taproom up to the community every weekend since they opened in 2013.

Beer Lover's Pick

Flying Mouse Five
Style: Pale Ale
ABV: 6.0%
Availability: Year-round
A nice balanced pale ale, the Flying Mouse Five is "Bartleby's brew of choice," and more importantly, a very good reward after a day of outdoor adventures on the trails.

PARKWAY BREWING

739 Kessler Mill Rd., Salem, VA 24153; (540) 314-8234; parkwaybrewing.com;
@ParkwayBrewing

Founded: 2012 **Founders:** Mike "Keno" and Lezlie Snyder **Brewer:** Ryan Worthington
Flagship Beers: Get Bent Mountain IPA, Majestic Mullet Krispy Kölsch, Bridge Builder
Blonde, Raven's Roost Baltic Porter **Year-Round Beers:** Same as flagships **Seasonals/
Special Releases:** Factory Girl Session IPA, The Remedy Brown Ale, Puppy Dawg Tails,
For Lovers Only Imperial Stout **Tours:** Upon request/if staff is available **Taproom:** Thurs
and Fri, 4 to 8 p.m.; Sat, 3 to 8 p.m.; Sun, 2 to 6 p.m.

Less than 7 miles from downtown Roanoke and only a little more than 1 mile from I-81, Parkway Brewing is at a convenient spot. You'll want to make this slight detour if you're traveling north or south along the corridor. You may even want to stay for the night; there are now enough breweries and beer bars in the Roanoke region for your own self-guided pub crawl.

Co-founder Mike "Keno" Snyder, along with his wife, Lezlie, spent years watching the growth of the craft beer movement, and had a firsthand view of it through his good friends at Breckenridge Brewery in Denver, Colorado. After a career in audio engineering, he decided to transition into the brewing world, where he first worked for a local brewery in Roanoke before deciding to open one himself.

The small community of Salem turned out to be the ideal spot to open his 30-barrel brewhouse. That brewhouse is led by brewmaster Ryan Worthington, who has a Seibel degree in brewing science, additional training qualifications from Doemens Academy in Munich, and has won multiple awards for beers he's been brewing since he started doing it at the age of 19.

Beer Lover's Pick

Get Bent Mountain IPA
Style: India Pale Ale
ABV: 7.2%
Availability: Year-round on tap and in bottles
A lighter-bodied West Coast–style IPA, this is an easy-drinking, not overly bitter choice. Enjoyable citrus flavors with a fairly smooth finish make this a beer you'll want to experience for yourself.

Ryan brews beers today like the **Bridge Builder Blonde**, a Belgian-style ale with a wheat-flavored base, and seasonals like the **For Lovers Only Imperial Stout**, a strong 9.5% beer that pays homage to the band Southern on the Skids from Chapel Hill, North Carolina.

Bands perform often at Parkway Brewing, where the large spacious warehouse interior is wide open and exposed, with plenty of room for the brew tanks, the bar, and lots of seating throughout. In addition to music, there are other cultural events like book readings and signings, and big events like a recent Oyster Roast, a 5-hour event that included performances from three different bands and food from Rappahannock River Oysters and Bruno's Gastro food truck.

Keno and the Parkway Brewing team hope to create more of a community feel, a hanging-out spot, a place where there are purposely no televisions so you can concentrate on socializing with your friends and neighbors at the bar.

QUEEN CITY BREWING
834 Springhill Rd., Staunton, VA 24401; (540) 213-8014; qcbrewing.com; @qcbrewing
Founded: 2004 (Brew-on-premise), 2013 (Brewery) **Founder:** Greg Ridenour **Brewer:** Greg Ridenour **Flagship Beer:** N/A **Year-Round Beers:** Gypsy Gold Ale, Munich Lager, Brass Knuckle IPA, King Rabbit Imperial IPA, Raspberry Wheat, Apricot White Rabbit, and Daddy Rabbit Stout **Seasonals/Special Releases:** Black Rabbit, Maibock, Winter Warmer, Jackalope IPA **Tours:** No **Taproom:** Tues to Thurs, 4 to 10 p.m.; Fri, 4 p.m. to 12 a.m.; Sat, 12 p.m. to 12 a.m.; Sun, 1 to 5 p.m.

Beginning as a brew-on-premise business, Queen City Brewing was created to inspire others to brew their own beer and learn how to do it onsite at their facility. Today there are a number of brew-on-premise options that often also intertwine with brewing the beer that you'll be able to taste onsite at the tasting room.

You can still brew your own private batch in 15-gallon batches, where you get to choose from a recipe of 80 different beers and brew it yourself onsite, then come back to bottle it a few weeks later. Queen City has also partnered with Blue Ridge Community College to offer two brewing courses.

Then there's a third option called the Brewer's Apprentice that takes place on Saturdays. For a fee of $35, you'll get your own tasting tray and get to watch the master brewer in action (and occasionally help) as you watch him make the beer and teach you his methods. At the end of the day, you'll also get a sixpack to take along with you.

Beer Lover's Pick

Black Rabbit Stout
Style: Stout
ABV: 5.3%
Availability: Rotating on tap
A great take on an Irish stout, the Black Rabbit is dark black in color and a nice combination of hoppy and rich and malty.

The beer you watch the master brewer make will eventually be one of the 22 taps on draft, including options like the **Bavarian Bock**, a nice dark 5.5% ABV lager, and the **Brass Knuckle IPA**, dry-hopped with a generous portion of Cascade hops.

Its beginnings as a brew-on-premise facility are evident when you enter Queen City Brewing because the first thing you see are the tanks front and center. Containers filled with grains and liquid extracts are on shelves on each side of the tanks. The tasting room area is basically built in behind and around the brew tanks as the key centerpiece.

There are dartboards to the right of the brew tanks, tables and a large projector TV screen to the left of the tanks, and behind the tanks there's a bar. All in all, it's a comfy, industrial space that gives you the chance to have a beer and also get a little better understanding of how it all happens, whether you're here for one of the beer events or just having a beer and getting the chance for a closeup look at all the beer ingredients and brew tanks.

REDBEARD BREWING COMPANY

120 S. Lewis St., Staunton, VA 24401; (804) 641-9340; redbeardbrews.com; @RedBeardBrews

Founded: 2013 **Founders:** Jonathan and Fara Wright **Brewer:** Jonathan Wright **Flagship Beers:** N/A **Year-Round Beers:** N/A **Seasonals/Special Releases:** All beers are small batch releases; Batch #42 Strong Ale, Watson Barleywine, Session IPA, Deep Luscious Amber (see website) **Tours:** No **Taproom:** See website for hours.

Based in the historic downtown Staunton area, Redbeard Brewing is convenient for tourists and residents taking in the downtown sights. Founders and

Black Rye IPA
Style: India Pale Ale
ABV: 7.5%
Availability: Special release
This deep black IPA has a full-bodied taste due to the hints of rye and the nice hop combination, while you still get the wonderful malty richness throughout.

husband-and-wife team Jonathan and Fara self-funded the business and believe in the concept that "bigger is not better." They strive to maintain complete control and keep things small and manageable, while also working to serve their local community and provide them with a nice laid-back environment in downtown Staunton to sample their beer.

That beer includes everything from flagship styles like their **America's Pale Ale** beer, English milds and bitters like the **Irene English Dark Mild** at 4.0% ABV, and the **A.M.O.G. Stout**, a milk stout made with coffee from Lucas Roasting Company in Virginia.

ROANOKE RAILHOUSE BREWERY

3106 Franklin Rd. SW, Roanoke, VA 24014; (540) 293-2423; roanokerailhouse.com; @RkeRailhouse

Founded: 2009 **Founder:** Steve Davidson **Brewer:** Tom Bradley **Flagship Beer:** Track 1 **Year-Round Beers:** Track 1, Switch Monkey, Broken Knuckle **Seasonals/Special Releases:** Conductor's Choice, Broken Knuckle IPA w/Blood Orange Infusion **Tours:** No **Taproom:** Mon to Fri, 4 to 8 p.m.; Sat and Sun, 2 to 7 p.m.

Enter the Roanoke Railhouse tasting room and the first thing you'll see is a framed poster of a rail yard. Study that poster from Roanoke artist Adam Johnson and you'll be able to connect the dots that carry over to Roanoke Railhouse's theme and slogan, "Take to the Rails." There's a *porter*, carrying luggage for the customers. A sign that reads *Track 1*. There's a *conductor* in the picture, and then other less obvious things, like the *knuckle*, a type of coupler that connects the vehicles of the train together.

Now take a look at their beer menu: Choose from beers like the **Broken Knuckle**, an English-style IPA that uses six different kinds of hops to achieve a nice hop aroma and flavor. Or try the **Conductor's Choice**, one of their seasonals, a rich chocolate stout. President and founder Steve Davidson believes in a strong marketing strategy and has developed his beer around this plan. Before he opened he spent a great deal of time investing in focus groups to help determine what their flagship beer would be. That beer is their **Track 1** amber lager.

They originally made this beer in a 1940s building that for many years was a Dr Pepper bottling plant. Steve was a real estate agent who for many years tried to convince clients that this old bottling plant would be the perfect brewery, until, as he told me, he finally convinced himself.

Today Steve has made some major operational changes and moved from that old bottling plant to a smaller industrial building near downtown Roanoke that houses the simple, comfortable tasting room and a 10-gallon system. Most of the beer—after it has been developed—is then produced at a larger Central Virginia brewery (contract-brewing arrangement). He explained that this concept has thus far worked extremely well for them, and allows their beer to be more easily distributed throughout the Commonwealth of Virginia.

At the tasting room, you'll still be able to sample a couple of their signature beers or enjoy a pint, as well as take home growlers or bottled beer to go.

Beer Lover's Pick

Track 1
Style: Munich Dunkel Lager
ABV: 4.58%
Availability: Year-round
The color pours a deep amber, tempting all those who prefer a malty variety of beer. It's sweet yet balanced, a session beer that's nice to drink in any season.

SEVEN ARROWS BREWING COMPANY

2508 Jefferson Hwy., #1, Waynesboro, VA 22980; (540) 221-6968;
sevenarrowsbrewing.com; @sevenarrowsbrew
Founded: 2014 **Founders:** Aaron and Melissa Allen **Brewer:** Aaron Allen **Flagship
Beer:** Eventide IPA **Year-Round Beers:** Eventide IPA, Sinistral Wheat, Aurora Pils,
Boreal Amber **Seasonals/Special Releases:** Kriophoros Bock, The Witching Hour Black
Lager, Cimmerian Black IPA, Spindrift Maibock, Oktoberfest, Hermenator Doppelbock
Tours: Sat, at designated times (see website) **Taproom:** Mon, 4 to 9 p.m.; Wed and
Thurs, 4 to 10 p.m.; Fri and Sat, 12 to 11 p.m.; Sun, 12 to 9 p.m. (hours change
seasonally)

Husband-and-wife team Aaron and Melissa Allen each have unique skills that
have equipped them with the needed tools for brewery ownership. As the Seven
Arrows head brewer, Aaron graduated with a degree in chemical engineering, then
worked at MillerCoors for almost 7 years as an engineer while simultaneously pursu-
ing courses to obtain a master's in brewing. Melissa received her MBA from James
Madison University and is fulfilling the business roles necessary in operating a brewery, like marketing, PR, and customer service management.

Shenandoah Valley

Eventide IPA
Style: India Pale Ale
ABV: 7.3%
Availability: Year-round on tap

One of their flagship beers, this IPA is love at first sight when you first notice its deep amber color and white head. The combination of Simcoe and Chinook hops give it a spicy flavor and unique character, making this beer a very good choice when you're pining for an American IPA.

Melissa also took a large role in designing the tasting room's look, geared to have a "cozy, warm and inviting feel." Events like comedy nights and music nights, along with food trucks outside, help to bring in customers to this location along the Jefferson Highway in Waynesboro. There's a separate private area with couches and a big TV that's often conveniently used as a kids' room on Sunday when parents and friends all get together for a beer.

Aaron strives to maintain balance in his beers and create them as "true to style" as he can on their 15-barrel brew system. You can find their beer at some restaurants and bars in nearby towns like Staunton and throughout Waynesboro, but the tasting room is where you should come to taste them all. With 12 beers on tap, you're in for an enjoyable tasting session. From those 12 beers, you'll be able to try their four core varieties, such as the **Sinistral Wheat**, a light gold Bavarian-style wheat beer, and the **Boreal Amber** beer, a deep amber ale with caramel hints. You'll be able to sample some of their seasonal releases and some "lab taps" (more experimental batches like a recent **Coffee Infused Pilsner**). Meanwhile, they're developing a Crooked Arrow series that will showcase a fruit lambic beer once a year. In summer 2016, look out for a blueberry lambic that will be aged for 13 months in a wine barrel.

SHENANDOAH VALLEY BREWING COMPANY

1700 Middlebrook Ave., Suite 300, Staunton, VA 24401; (540) 887-2337;
shenvalbrew.com; @shevalbrew
Founded: 2014 **Founder:** Mike "Chappy" Chapple **Brewer:** Mike "Chappy" Chapple,
Edan Valker **Flagship Beers:** 1st Brigade Red IPA, Virginia Native Amber Ale **Beers:**
(approx. 70% are recurring) Buck 'N Ball American Brown Ale, 1st Brigade Red IPA, Aus
Dem Tal Altbier, Beverly Light Ale, Bent Brethren Belgian Abbey, BlueGrass Blended Ale,
Spottswood Stout (see website for specifics) **Tours:** No **Taproom:** Thurs, 12 to 9 p.m.;
Fri and Sat., 12 to 11 p.m.; Sun, 12 to 6 p.m.

When you're in the mood for some good "craic," consider a visit to Shenandoah Valley Brewing Company in downtown Staunton. "Craic" is the Gaelic word for fun and enjoyment, and at this brewery, that's what the tasting room atmosphere is meant to re-create—the feeling of hanging out at an Irish pub. Though you won't find Guinness here, you can often get a stout or porter-style beer, like their rich, malty **Spottswood Stout.**

You can also get some German styles such as the **Schonen Weizen** brewed with German Weizen beer yeast or the **Aus Dem Tal Altbier** that uses German grains, yeast, and hops and an old-world brewing process to mimic the same beer you might try in Dusseldorf, Germany. Or opt for the balanced **Buck 'N Ball American**

Beer Lover's Pick

1st Brigade Red IPA
Style: India Pale Ale
ABV: 8%
Availability: Recurring/mostly year-round
A deep red color and bright hop notes are present in
this red IPA–style beer. At 8% ABV, it's both strong and
hoppy, but also has the balance created by the caramel
grains and other malts used to even it all out.

Brown Ale, a combination of American brown ale attributes rounded out using some English-style hops.

Whether it's English, German, Belgian, American, or otherwise, you'll have a variety of beer to choose from with an average of 14 taps available at the tasting room, housed in an old building in downtown Staunton. Though it's not as old as some Irish pubs you may find in Ireland, the building has its own great history. It was once an old grain mill warehouse.

Founder Mike "Chappy" set up a homebrew supply store in this building in 2012. In years since he's expanded into the Irish bar and the 2-barrel nanobrewery that you'll find inside today. The homebrew store is also still successfully running in an adjacent shop next to the tasting room (see BYOB: Brew Your Own Beer section).

SOARING RIDGE CRAFT BREWERS

523 Shenandoah Ave., Roanoke, VA 24016; (540) 529-2140; soaringridge.com;
@soaringridge

Founded: 2014 **Founders:** Nathan Hungate, Sean Osborne, Michael Barnes **Brewer:**
Sean Osborne **Flagship Beers:** Virginia Creeper Ale, Trailhead Nut Brown Ale **Year-
Round Beers:** Tinker Crek Kölsch, White Top White Ale, Virginia Creeper American
Pale Ale, Switchback IPA, Trailhead Nut Brown Ale, Twisted Stump Porter **Seasonals/
Special Releases:** Night Hiker Black IPA, Rum Raisin Oak, Saison, Oktoberfest **Tours:** No
Taproom: Wed to Fri, 4 to 9 p.m.; Sat, 2 to 9 p.m.

An open-air concept was the driver behind the Soaring Ridge founders' decision
to open their 7-barrel brewhouse in downtown Roanoke. Garage doors extend
the length of their brewery and tasting room and open up during warm days. There

Beer Lover's Pick

Trailhead Nut Brown Ale
Style: Nut Brown Ale
ABV: 6%
Availability: Year-round on tap
Nutty, malty and sweet, this brown ale combines UK and US attributes to create a
nice light- to medium-bodied brown ale. English hops add a touch of bitterness to
enhance the sweetness.

are two levels of platforms with tables and a good-sized bar on the elevated platform. The brew tanks are all visible behind the platforms.

During my visit they had a very serious cornhole tournament going on, a usual weekly event with a few different matches taking place simultaneously. Cornhole matches deserve a beer. For a refreshing one, try the **Tinker Creek Kolsch**, a light-bodied straw gold beer brewed with German malts and hops. Or maybe the **White Top White Ale**, with some citrusy and spicy flavors from the coriander, orange peel, and chamomile.

SWOVER CREEK FARMS—FARM BREWERY
4176 Swover Creek Rd., Edinburg, VA 22824; (540) 984-8973; swovercreekfarms.com
Founded: 2014 **Founders:** Dave and Lynn St. Clair **Brewers:** Dave and Lynn St. Clair, Curtis Falkenstein **Flagship Beer:** Light Ale (made with different kinds of single hop varieties from the farm) **Year-Round Beers:** Dirty Blonde Ale, Columbia Furnace Ale, Cabin Creek Coffee Stout (subject to change) **Seasonals/Special Releases:** Wheat Ale, Rye IPA, Oatmeal Porter, Black IPA **Tours:** No **Taproom:** Fri, 3 to 7:30 p.m.; Sat and Sun, 12 to 7 p.m.

Swover Creek Farms has existed for over 100 years—a century farm. Lynn and Dave St. Clair took over the ownership from Lynn's grandfather in the '90s and bought the adjacent property, making it a combined property of over 200 acres.

Rye IPA
Style: IPA
ABV: 7.4%
Availability: Rotating on tap

This IPA is evenly balanced while at the same time imparting that crisp nutty flavor from the use of rye in their malt bill. It's easy to have more than one.

Though this farm has existed for a long time, it hasn't always had as many things going on as it does today. There are cattle and sheep, an egg and chicken ranch, and a kitchen where they now sell some fresh foods and baked goods like smoked sausages, pierogies, empanadas, cakes, and cookies. There's a successful pick-your-own berry business that Lynn began in 1998, and a hop yard that they added in 2013.

And as of 2014, there's now a brewery. "The brewery concept never came up, it just appeared," co-founder Dave St. Clair explains to me. Originally the idea was to expand the pick-your-own business plan. Instead of just berries, they'd also create a pick-your-own hops operation for the many homebrewers in the area. After visiting breweries around Virginia, David and Lynn began to notice a trend; you didn't need to have a large brewing operation in place to establish a brewery. They loved the nanobrewery concept and thought they could add this business to their already existing businesses on the farm.

Enter the farm brewery today and you'll find an average of 4 beers on tap, where you can buy a pint, a flight, or a growler. Experience the taste of different hops by trying the **Light Ale**, part of their Hopyard Series where they use the same base ale and pair it with a single hop they grow on the farm like Chinook, Cascade, or Columbus. Try the **Dirty Blonde**, named because it's a standard blonde ale that's a little darker in color (during one brew they mistakenly put a little darker malt into the recipe but it still tasted great). For a darker option, there's usually the **Cabin Creek Coffee Stout** on tap, made with coffee beans that they get from their neighbor who's a coffee roaster.

You can enjoy your beer at the small bar on the main floor, or head upstairs where there's a bookshelf filled with a variety of books and guides, a few tables, and some comfortable cushioned seating on the chairs or on the couch. If you decide after this pleasant experience that you want to become a more regular customer, then consider joining the "Farmer of the Ale mug club," where for a one-time fee you get an extra 4 ounces of beer in every pint, a discount on growlers, and your own custom-designed mug. A potter also happens to be one of their neighbors, and she'll design the mug of your choice.

The brewery side of their business is growing. Dave and Lynn have recently hired brewer Curtis Falkenstein to create some new recipes, and their current 20-gallon brew system will soon be upgraded to a 5-barrel system. They're in the process of converting the barn next door to a taproom and brewhouse, along with covered outdoor seating and a beer garden. Expect to see this by sometime in 2016.

THREE NOTCH'D BREWING, HARRISONBURG

241 E. Market St., Harrisonburg, VA 22801; (540) 217-5939; threenotchdbrewing .com; @ThreeNotchdBeer

Founded: 2013 **Founders:** Scott Roth, George Kastendike, Derek Naughton **Brewers:** Dave Warwick, Mary Morgan **Flagship Beers:** 40-Mile IPA, Hydraulion Red **Year-Round Beers:** 40 Mile IPA, Hydraulion Red, The Ghost, No Veto **Seasonals/Special Releases:** Farmers Pale Ale, Hansel and Kettle Imperial Oktoberfest, Biggie Smores Imperial Stout (see website for full list) **Tours:** No **Taproom:** Tues and Wed, 4 to 10 p.m.; Thurs, 4 to 11 p.m.; Fri, 3 p.m. to midnight; Sat, 12 p.m. to midnight; Sun, 2 to 10 p.m.

The success of the original Three Notch'd Brewing brewery based in Charlottesville has enabled them to open this second great spot in downtown Harrisonburg. The atmosphere, like its Charlottesville spot, is relaxed, laid-back and both kid friendly and pet friendly. Communal long tables and various areas with couches and comfy chairs fill the tasting room.

Though all the main brewing happens in Charlottesville (see Central Virginia chapter), the Harrisonburg location is equipped with a ½ barrel nanobrewery system that enables them to offer experimental and innovative beers that you can only get here at this location.

They're working hard on collaborating with other brewers, and they offer a series of beers that do just that, like the **Midnight Vortex**, a black IPA brewed in collaboration with Sedona Taphouse (see Multilocation Brewpubs & Beer Bars section) of Charlottesville. Or maybe opt for the **Hysteria Imperial India Brown Ale** brewed in collaboration with Devils Backbone Brewing Company. At the bar, you

can custom design your own tasting by picking from a board of labeled bottle caps. These caps are then placed on wooden cutting board–style tasting trays next to each beer of your choosing.

Beer Lover's Pick

"No Veto" English Brown Ale
Style: Brown Ale
ABV: 5.0%
Availability: Year-round on tap

Caramel and toffee flavors rouse your taste buds in this malty but smooth English-style brown ale made with English malts. Just the right amount of hops add a touch of bitterness at the finish. It pours a rich brown color and tastes smooth and malty. At a sessionable 5% ABV, it's a refreshing change from strong, sweet, and overly bitter high-ABV craft beers you see more often in today's craft beer industry.

Beer Bars

BLUE 5 RESTAURANT
312 Second St., Roanoke, VA 24011; (540) 904-5338; blue5restaurant.com;
Draft Beers: 46 **Bottled/Canned Beers:** 50+

Established in 2007, Blue 5's concept is a "5-star restaurant where family and friends can enjoy world-class craft beer, live music and exceptional Southern cuisine in historic downtown Roanoke." There were 16 beers on tap when they opened, mostly all craft beer–centric, and a few years later that tripled to 46 beers on tap. That craft beer menu is a beautiful sight to see as you take a seat at the L-shaped bar or at one of the restaurant tables.

Many of those tables also offer a great view of the stage (live music events occasionally take place here—check out the events calendar on their website). Even if you're there on a non-event night, you're in for a treat with the exceptional food menu and probably what you're visiting for if you're reading this book: amazing craft beer.

The beer menu is clear and easy to follow, grouped in categories like Wheats & Lighter Stuff, Ambers-Lagers, Pale Ales, Belgians, and The Dark Side—Stouts, Porters, and Browns. Their craft beer selection has put them on beer lovers' radar, particularly in recent years when they made Craftbeer.com's list for the Top 25 Best Beer Bars in America.

In addition to all the unique craft beer from other parts of the US and the rest of the world, there's also always a good selection of beer from local Virginia breweries. This list rotates regularly and you should also be on the lookout for beer events and tap takeover nights.

Harrisonburg—Pub Crawl

Home to two universities, James Madison University and Eastern Mennonite University, downtown Harrisonburg is an enjoyable area to walk around, not only for a pub crawl but also because it was named one of the Great American Main Streets in the US in 2014. An organization, Harrisonburg Downtown Renaissance, was formed in 2004 to reinvigorate the area, investing in historic run-down buildings and attracting businesses to the downtown. Today that downtown includes a number of great beer bars and breweries.

You can either choose to visit three or four beer spots on this pub crawl. The first option will give you a little more exercise—physical activity combined with some great beer. Those inclined to do less walking should go with option two.

Option 1: Begin at Brothers Craft Brewing and visit a total of four spots. Total walking distance = approximately 1 mile. Or Option 2: Begin at the second stop, Capital Ale House, and visit a total of three spots. Total walking distance = approximately .4 mile.

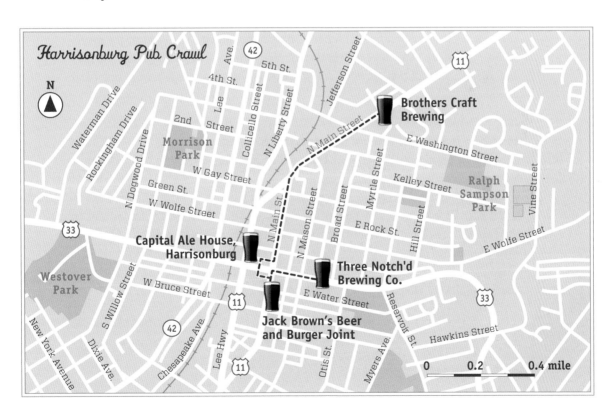

Brothers Craft Brewing, 800 N. Main St., Harrisonburg, VA 22802; (540) 421-6599; brotherscraftbrewing.com. Once a Coca-Cola bottling plant, this warehouse brewery is a great place to begin your pub crawl. Order a flight, check out the brewery through the glass windows of the tasting room, and get a snack if you're hungry at one of the food carts usually parked outside.

Head southwest on N. Main Street toward E. Washington Street. Walk for about .8 mile until you get to Court Square. Turn right on Court Square and you will see Capital Ale House at the northwest corner of the square.

Capital Ale House, 41-A Court Square, Harrisonburg, VA 22801; (540) 564-ALES; capitalalehouse.com. Capital Ale House's popularity and reputation in Virginia is obvious, with its now five locations throughout the state. There's a good reason for all of this—there's an amazing beer selection, quality service, and great food. With an average of over 60 beers on draft, the menu might be a little overwhelming at first, but the staff and the category descriptions will help you to narrow it down. This is a good stop to get a snack or some food to get you through the rest of the pub crawl, but also remember the next stop is a burger joint for those craving a juicy burger with their beer.

Head south on Court Square. Follow Court Square around until you come to the southeast corner, where you'll take a right onto S. Main Street. You'll see Jack Brown's Beer and Burger Joint on the left hand side (east side) of the street less than one block down.

Jack Brown's Beer and Burger Joint, 80 S. Main St., Harrisonburg, VA 22801; (540) 443-5225; jackbrownsjoint.com The bar's catch phrase explains it all—a "burger joint with a passion for craft beer." This joint in Harrisonburg is one of four Virginia locations, but the Harrisonburg one is the original. It's tiny and compact but if you're lucky enough to secure one of the seats at the bar, you may find it hard to leave. Jack Brown's Beer and Burger Joint has a dive bar feel, with decorations in the form of tires hanging from the ceiling, a stack of bras, and a disco ball. Along with your choice of over 100 craft beers, you can get a basic burger or a more eclectic burger, like the Jack on Piggy Back, a burger topped with a split and griddled hot dog, with pickled jalapenos and cheddar cheese.

Head north on S. Main Street (take a right out of the Jack Brown's exit) toward Court Square. Turn right on E. Market Street and walk about 3 blocks. Your final beer stop will be on the right hand side of the street.

Three Notch'd Brewing, 241 E. Market St., Harrisonburg, VA 22801; (540) 217-5939; threenotchdbrewing.com The final stop on your pub crawl is also a great hangout spot, so if you feel like staying for more than one beer, the atmosphere at Three Notch'd may give you the perfect excuse, especially if you're able to claim the couch or comfortable seating options in the corner. Three Notch'd Brewing Company's original brewery is in Charlottesville, but this brewery location has its own nano-system for some creative and unique batches that you can only get in Harrisonburg.

Staunton—Pub Crawl

Staunton is a charming, historic town in the middle of the Shenandoah Valley region. This pub crawl allows you to take in the scene in the downtown area and takes you to a small residential area outside of the central downtown community. The total walking distance from the first to the last stop is approximately 1 mile.

Queen City Brewing, 834 Springhill Rd., Staunton, VA 24401; (540) 213-8014; qcbrewing.com. A short trip from the historic downtown Staunton center, Queen City Brewing is a relaxed brewpub as well as a brew-on-premise operation. If you plan it out correctly, you can start your day by doing some hands-on brewing and learning yourself while you enjoy one of their beers onsite—they have 22 taps, so plenty to choose from!

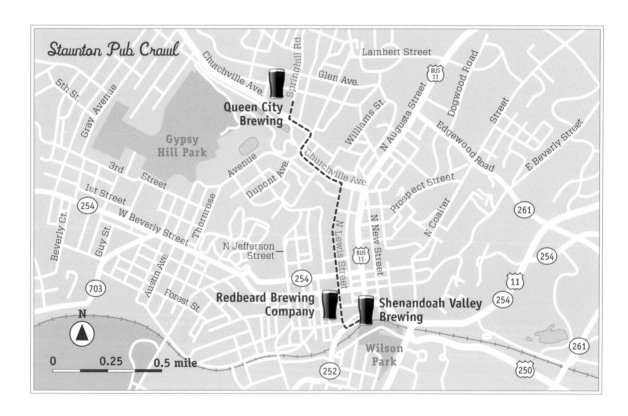

Head south on Springhill Road toward Churchville Avenue. Turn left on Churchville Avenue. After a little less than a half mile, turn right onto N. Lewis Street and follow N. Lewis for .6 mile. Your next beer stop will be on the right hand side.

Redbeard Brewing Company, 120 S. Lewis St., Staunton, VA 24401; (804) 641-9340; redbeardbrews.com This nanobrewery operation run and funded solely by husband-and-wife team Jonathan and Fara Wright has a motto of "Small Batches of Big Brews." The tasting room is simple and relaxed.

Take a right when you leave Redbeard Brewing (head south in the direction of Federal Street). A very short walk later, you'll take a left onto Middlebrook Avenue. Shenandoah Valley Brewing Company will be on your left.

Shenandoah Valley Brewing Company, 17 Middlebrook Ave., Suite 300, Staunton, VA 24401; (540) 887-2337; shenvalbrew.com. Shenandoah Valley Brewing Company, located in the heart of downtown Staunton, is a good place to end your pub crawl and move on to other eating or shopping establishments nearby. If your experience earlier on in the pub crawl at Queen City Brewing sparked your desire to try home-brewing beer yourself, you can buy the supplies you'll need at the homebrew store connected to the brewery.

Coastal Virginia

Plenty of tourists flock to coastal Virginia every year. Sometimes that's for a taste of history at Colonial Williamsburg. Sometimes it's for the beach, the chance to relax in the sun and partake in the entertainment.

Today it's also for the beer. The coastal Virginia region is establishing its own footprint in the state's beer scene, but keep in mind that this is a beer scene that is quickly changing day by day. It's highly likely the number of breweries will have doubled in the coming months, with close to 10 new breweries already targeted for opening in the near future.

Coastal Virginia has a lot of things going for it, and even the beer experts seem to have noticed that, as a reputable San Diego Brewery, Green Flash Brewing, recently started construction and planning for a new 58,000-square-foot facility, with a 100,000-barrel brewhouse, in Virginia Beach.

Breweries

ALEWERKS BREWING COMPANY

189-B Ewell Rd., Williamsburg, VA 23188; (757) 220-3670; alewerks.com; @alewerks

Founded: 2006 **Founder:** Chuck Haines **Brewer:** Geoff Logan **Flagship Beer:** Chesapeake Pale Ale **Year-Round Beers:** Chesapeake Pale Ale, Wheat Ale, Red Marker Ale, Washington's Porter, Drake Tail Ale IPA, Tavern Ale **Seasonals/Special Releases:** Pumpkin Ale, White Ale, Coffeehouse Stout, Bitter Valentine, Bourbon Barrel Porter, Café Royale (see website for more) **Tours:** Mon to Fri, 4:30 p.m.; Sat, 3:30 and 4:30 p.m.; call to reserve in advance **Taproom:** Mon to Thurs, 12 to 7 p.m.; Fri and Sat., 12 to 8 p.m.; Sun, 12 to 5 p.m. (see website for specifics, hours to be extended in near future)

Based only a short few miles away from Colonial Williamsburg, Alewerks is conveniently on the way to and from many attractions in this region, an easy stopover to add to your travel itinerary.

After a day of touring the Revolutionary City, you may want to try Alewerks signature beers like the **Washington's Porter**, an American-style porter with a lot of rich and roasted dark malts, or the **Tavern Ale**, a palatable malty brown ale.

Beer Lover's Pick

My Bitter Valentine
Style: Double IPA
ABV: 8.3%
Availability: Limited release
Part of the Alewerks Brewermaster Reserve series, this beer is a coveted double IPA that's packed with Pacific Northwest hops and available in 22-ounce bottles. One to look to purchase during your visit to the tasting room.

Brewmaster Geoff Logan has been running things at Alewerks Brewing since 2008 and has developed a reputation for making great, crowd-pleasing beers that are now distributed throughout Virginia, Washington, DC, and parts of North Carolina.

When you visit the tasting room, you'll often get the chance to try some of the more eclectic small batch recipes that Alewerks tests out as they experiment with new kinds of beers, such as the **Café Royal**, a bourbon barrel–aged milk stout that received a 95 out of a 100 rating on the *Beer Advocate* review site from fans.

Along with a gift shop, the tasting room also has a wraparound bar that's comfortable for drinking the 17 beers on tap including a cask ale option. Plans are in the works to include an outdoor patio and possibly offer a mug club for tasting room regulars in the coming months.

BACK BAY BREWING COMPANY
614 Norfolk Ave., Virginia Beach, VA 23451; (757) 531-7750; backbaybrewingco
.com
Founded: 2012 **Founders:** Josh Canada, Charlie Burroughs, George Powell **Brewers:** See founders' names **Flagship Beer:** False Cape Amber Ale **Year-Round Beers:** False Cape Amber Ale, Steel Pier Lager, Atlantic Ave IPA **Seasonals/Special Releases:** The Witch of Pungo, Lynnhaven River Oyster Stout, Nut Quacker **Tours:** Upon request **Taproom:** Tues to Thurs, 3 to 10 p.m.; Fri and Sat, 12 p.m. to 12 a.m.; Sun, 12 to 8 p.m.

Three childhood friends came together to create this hangout tasting room in Virginia Beach. Upon entering, your eyes will probably be drawn to the nano-brew system to your left, squeezed into this storefront shop along Norfolk Avenue.

Reclaimed wood and a white-painted wall look on the interior, along with duck and fish decorations on the walls, makes it feel laid back and beachy. At the bar, you can taste beer to stick with the beach theme, like the **Beach Cruiser Pale Ale**, a mix between an American- and English-style ale. You can also sample one of their original offerings, the **False Cape Ale**, medium bodied with enough bitterness to taste but still balanced. An upstairs space with darts and a small window overlooks

the first floor action, and if you're in the mood for food there's a taco joint next door where you can easily get food, then bring it back to enjoy with your flight of beer.

For the larger batches, the Back Bay team partner-brews (also known as contract brewing) with another brewery outside of Virginia Beach, but plans are in the works for their own brewing facility in the future.

Beer Lover's Pick

Steel Pier Bohemian Lager
Style: Lager
ABV: 4.7%
Availability: Seasonal on tap
This beer is light bodied, crisp, and, a nice version of a Munich Helles–style lager. A classic beer to drink on a classic day at the beach.

BIG UGLY BREWING COMPANY

1296 South Battlefield Blvd., Suite 104, Chesapeake, VA 23322; (757) 609-2739; biguglybrewing.com; @BigUglyBrewing

Founded: 2015 **Founders:** Jim and Michele Lantry, Shawn and Aaron Childers **Brewers:** Jim Lantry, Evan Lantry, Darrell Cuenca **Flagship Beer:** Ape Hanger Russian Imperial Stout **Year-Round Beers:** Sunbeam Blonde Ale, Split Window Saison, Rockers IPA, Ape Hanger Russian Imperial Stout, Ghost Rider Porter, Magic Berliner Bus **Seasonals/Special Releases:** Belgian Wit, Steady As She Gose (see website for more) **Tours:** Upon request **Taproom:** Wed and Thurs, 5 to 9 p.m.; Fri, 5 to 10 p.m.; Sat. 12 to 10 p.m.; Sun, 12 to 4 p.m.

The town of Chesapeake, Virginia, where Big Ugly Brewing Company is based, once ranked as the third most boring city in the country, according to a list by Movoto Real Estate. Co-founders Jim Lantry and Shawn Childers are doing their part in changing their city's reputation with the opening of Big Ugly Brewing Company in early 2015. Chesapeake now has its own community pub.

With a tasting room designed in a garage theme, it's minimalistic while also displaying a variety of cool features. Inside an actual garage, you'd expect to see a

vehicle like a car or a truck, but inside the brewery you get to admire vintage British motorcycles from Shawn's personal collection. One customer seating table even uses a motorcycle seat in place of a barstool. This theme carries over to the brewery's name, too, which was named after Shawn's 1955 restored Chevy truck that's been nicknamed Big Ugly from the time he brought the truck home. You can see a picture of the truck on the brewery's wall.

The main attraction as you enter is a yellow VW mini bus that looks like it's straight out of *That 70s Show*. The interior of the bus has been converted to a private seating area for customers. There are a few seats and a table made out of beer bottle caps, as well as a TV that plays the movie *Endless Summer* continuously. Customers can reserve the bus by calling in advance.

Though there's no food served, you can call in a delivery order from a 1950s phone booth, still fully functional, that's situated in between the VW mini bus and the brewery tanks. A spacious bar offers ample seating along with an assortment of tables, while the 7-barrel brewhouse and fermenters are all out in the open in the back half of the tasting room.

This 7-barrel system is put to hard work as Jim and the brewing team create beer like the **Steady As She Gose** beer, a Gose-style beer spiced up with ghost peppers, and the **Rockers IPA**, made with a whopping 9 pounds of citrusy hops. Their beer glasses describe the theme they're going for: "Big. Bold. Beer." Barrel-aged beers are in planning for limited release in the fall and winter.

Beer Lover's Pick

Ape Hanger Russian Imperial Stout
Style: Imperial Stout
ABV: 9.5%
Availability: Year-round on tap
Big Ugly Brewing's focus on big, bold beers is evident in their flagship beer, an imperial stout filled with dark chocolatey, bold goodness from the deep black, patent and roasted barley malts and eight hop additions.

BRASS CANNON BREWING COMPANY

8105 Richmond Rd. #105, Toano, VA 23168; (757) 566-0001; brasscannonbrewing
.com; @BrassCannonBrew
Founded: 2012 **Founders:** Tony Artrip, Scott Kennedy, Phil Norfolk **Brewer:** Scott
Kennedy **Flagship Beer:** Angry Scot **Year-Round Beers:** Barrage Brown Ale, Angry
Scot, Muzzle Flash American Amber, Broadside IPA, Smoothbore Stout **Seasonals/
Special Releases:** St. Barbara Heather Ale, Split Shot, Kanonefest, Great Turkish
Bombard **Tours:** Upon request **Taproom:** Mon and Tues, 12 to 7 p.m.; Fri and Sat., 12 to
7 p.m.; Sun, 12 to 5 p.m.

Brass Cannon Brewing Company was formed by three friends who shared a love
for homebrewing. Founders Tony Artrip, Scott Kennedy, and Phil Norfolk realized they worked more effectively together as a group than each one did individually, and after brewing for a while together, began to put plans into place for a
nanobrewery of their own.

Toano, Virginia, was established as the location due to its convenience; it was a
good midpoint in driving distance from each of their homes, which at that time were
spread out between Williamsburg, Richmond, and Virginia Beach.

Once they decided on Toano, the region's historical past helped inspire the
brewery's name and their beer recipes, many of which are historically inspired or
sourced recipes, a combination of the "old world and new world," as Tony relays.

One of those is the **Broadside IPA**, which is a mixture between an English and
American IPA style, using American yeast and a blend of American and UK hops
with a medium light body. Or for those who enjoy the malty beers, sample the

Beer Lover's Pick

Angry Scot
Style: Scottish Strong Ale
ABV: 7.8%
Availability: Year-round on tap
This Scottish-style ale is sweet with flavors of caramel and
syrupy-like qualities from the use of black treacle, as well
as a hint of smoke. There's a slight amount of bitterness
from the English Kent Golding hops that are used in the
recipe to round it all out.

Smoothbore Stout, which is a more medium-bodied dark-colored ale that's brewed with Irish oats.

All of this beer is made on a 4-barrel system, with a lot of "boot-strapped equipment," much of which has been repurposed from other cooking or dairy equipment to make beer, such as the mash tun, which started its life as a dough fryer.

O'CONNOR BREWING COMPANY

211 W. 24th St., Norfolk, VA 23517; (757) 623-2337; oconnorbrewing.com; @OConnorBrewing

Founded: 2010 **Founders:** Kevin and Penny O'Connor **Brewer:** Kevin O'Connor (head brewer), Skylar Sickles, Bob Sweeney **Flagship Beer:** El Guapo IPA **Year-Round Beers:** El Guapo IPA, Norfolk Canyon Pale Ale, Great Dismal Black IPA, Green Can Golden Ale, Red Nun Red Ale, O'Connor's Dry Irish Stout (ODIS) **Seasonals/Special Releases:** Winter Pecan Porter, Punkelweizz, Lil' SIPA, Ibrik Turkish Coffee Imperial Stout (see website for specifics) **Tours:** Upon request **Taproom:** Tues to Thurs, 4 to 8 p.m.; Fri, 4 to 9 p.m.; Sat, 12 to 9 p.m.; Sun, 12 to 6 p.m. (Hours change seasonally; please see website for specifics.)

Drinking bad beer often defines many of our college drinking experiences, or more specifically, drinking the cheapest, most inexpensive beer meant for drinking out of plastic cups and using in a game of beer pong. Founder Kevin O'Connor wasn't drinking bad beer during his college years; he developed his love for craft beer early

while he was technically considered underage. While in college, he always shocked the local store owner with his purchases, who used to remark that he "never saw a college kid come in and buy so much good beer." From there the next logical progression was to start trying to make that same beer himself.

Years later, after spending countless hours researching the beer business, evaluating the cost of beer equipment, and brewing many beers in his own backyard, he knew it was time to make a change. After a stint at St. George Brewery and in the distribution business, Kevin's wife, Penny, convinced him to take the plunge. Many of Kevin's family members have pursued entrepreneurial paths; it was time for Kevin to follow suit.

The path of an entrepreneur seems to have been a smart choice! They began brewing on a 2-vessel, 10-barrel brew system, and today they're brewing on a 4-vessel, 30-barrel brew system. More and more fermenters have been purchased to increase their production. Their original brewery was a 5,000-square-foot facility, and in 2014 they moved a few blocks down the road to a much larger facility, seven times the square feet of their first facility, with 35,000 square feet of space.

It's no surprise that with all this square footage, their tasting room is equally massive—one of the largest tasting rooms in Virginia. They envisioned a tasting room that could also be used as an event space, and it regularly is used for events. There's live music, and a private event room on the second floor where you can overlook the brewhouse and the other public tasting rooms. One room on the main floor functions as a game area, with cornhole and board games available to play. Another room is adjacent to the brew tanks, filled with lots of picnic tables and overlooking

Beer Lover's Pick

El Guapo
Style: India Pale Ale
ABV: 7.5%
Availability: Year-round on tap and in bottles
Made with agave nectar, this IPA has some wonderful citrus flavors with a nice balance of bitterness. It pours a golden orange color with a frothy head, and is one of O'Connor Brewing's flagship brews.

the outside patio space. Both kid friendly and dog friendly, there's room for everyone. "The more the merrier," Penny confirms.

Their beer has developed a strong reputation among beer fans since they brewed their first beer on St. Patrick's Day 2010. Next St. Patrick's Day, you may want to consider the O'Connor beer style that will fit the bill, the **O'Connor's Dry Irish Stout (ODIS)**, a smooth full-bodied Irish stout that should please any Irishman. Or for a more medium-bodied variety, try the **Red Nun Red Ale**, malty with some light hops, a beautiful overall balance—and a gold medal winner at the 2014 Virginia Craft Brewers fest.

PLEASURE HOUSE BREWING
3025 Shore Dr., Virginia Beach, VA 23451; (757) 496-0916; pleasurehousebrewing .com; @pleasurehousebr
Founded: 2014 **Founders:** Tim O'Brien, Drew Stephenson, Alex Stephenson, Kevin Loos **Brewers:** Drew Stephenson, Bre Ingargiola **Flagship Beer:** N/A (will be defined in future months) **Beers:** Lesner Sunrise, Doctor in the House, Oregon Tourist 2.0, Lynnhaven Coffee Cream Stout, Halfway House, Sunken Truck (see website for specifics)
Tours: Upon request **Taproom:** Wed and Thurs, 3 to 10 p.m.; Fri, 3 to 11 p.m.; Sat, 12 to 11 p.m.; Sun, 12 to 10 p.m. (see website for specifics, extended hours in coming months)

Historians in the Virginia Beach area refer to an old tavern dating back to the 17th or 18th century called Pleasure House Tavern that served as a local gathering spot for the community—at least for the men in the community (women weren't permitted inside).

Beer Lover's Pick

Lesner Sunrise
Style: Belgian Single
ABV: 5.6%
Availability: Rotating
The sweetness of a Belgian-style ale with the addition of lemongrass makes this a bold sweet and spicy combination, while also light bodied and very sessionable at 5.6% ABV.

The Pleasure House Brewery is named after this old tavern, and though some things have changed in the 21st century—women are obviously welcome now—the Pleasure House brewing team hopes to serve the same purpose as the original tavern did—to be the local gathering spot for their community.

Based in a shopping plaza on a main thoroughfare in Virginia Beach, this nano-brewing operation is attracting its share of local residents. During the first 6 months of operating, they introduced close to 65 different beers on tap. Their 3.5-barrel setup is as manual as it comes, some of it repurposed from its original use as dairy equipment.

This setup also means there's always something new to try even if you're a regular customer. One of those options might be the **Halfway House**, a West Coast–style IPA, or the **Lynnhaven Coffee Cream Stout**, a sweet stout with flavors of vanilla, coffee, and chocolate. The only place you can try their beer is at the tasting room (for now), though they've recently ordered additional fermenters and in the near future may begin distribution to nearby restaurants and bars.

REAVER BEACH BREWING CO.

1505 Taylor Farm Rd., Virginia Beach, VA 23453; (757) 563-2337; reaverbeach.com;
@beachbrewing

Founded: 2010 **Founders:** Justin and Kristin MacDonald **Brewer:** Justin MacDonald
Flagship Beer: Hoptopus Double IPA **Year-Round Beers:** Hurricane American Wheat,
Riptide Altbier, Hammerhead IPA, Hoptopus Double IPA, Sea Devil Imperial Stout
Seasonals/Special Releases: Ghost Ship Citra Pale Ale, Oceanus Aurum Honey Rye
Saison, Sandshark Summer Kolsch, Jolly Roger Pumpkin Porter, Polaris Winter Tripel (see
website for more) **Tours:** Upon request **Taproom:** Tues to Thurs, 3 to 7 p.m.; Fri, 3 to 9
p.m.; Sat, 12 to 9 p.m.; Sun, 1 to 6 p.m.

From 12-gallon batches to 465-gallon batches, Reaver Beach Brewing has grown
since opening in a much smaller facility in 2010. The tasting room is both rustic
and modern, in warm colors of burgundy and browns with barrel cocktail tables. It's
meant for sampling, maybe drinking a pint or so, but Justin emphasizes that's it's
not a bar or a place to go when you want to be out all night partying, either. The
tasting room hours, open until 9 p.m. at the latest even on weekend nights, reflect
this choice.

It's meant for *tasting* and above all enjoying the flavors of the beer, and at
Reaver Beach Brewing, that ranges from very hop-forward American-style ales to
wild ales. Hop-forward beers might include some of their limited release beers like

Hoptopus
Style: Double IPA
ABV: 8.8%
Availability: Year-round on tap and in cans
Described as a hophead's dream, this double IPA is generously hopped multiple times during the boil, then dry-hopped some more, to achieve its over 100 bitterness level and 8.8% ABV.

The Kracken, a powerful 10.5% ABV triple IPA with 130 IBUs, or the **Hammerhead IPA**, one of their year-round beers that you will likely see on your visit to the taproom. They're working on a sour program that they're beginning to release to customers in the near future.

"It's a lifestyle," co-founder Justin MacDonald explains when asked about day-to-day life in the brewery business. Take a look at the Reaver Beach logo in closer detail to understand why; it's a spin on a "Jolly Roger" pirate flag, where you'll notice a hop cone and crossed mash paddles intertwined into the design. This may help signify the lifestyle that Justin abides by in both his career and the beer he's making; "It speaks to the rebellious nature in us and the voice in our head that demands we eschew the traditional path in favor of one far less certain, but far more exciting."

SMARTMOUTH BREWING COMPANY
1309 Raleigh Ave., Suite 300, Norfolk, VA 23507; (757) 624-3939;
smartmouthbrewing.com; @smartmouthbeer
Founded: 2012 **Founders:** The Hardys, The Neikirks, and friends **Brewer:** Greg Papp
Flagship Beer: Alter Ego Saison **Year-Round Beers:** Murphy's Law Amber Ale, Rule G IPA, Alter Ego Saison, Notch 9 Double IPA **Seasonals/Special Releases:** Sommer Fling Hefeweizen, Cowcatcher Milk Stout, Outta Yer Gourd Pumpkin Ale, Holiday Helper Imperial Red, Bandwagon (see website for more) **Tours:** Sat, hourly tours starting at 2:15 p.m.
Taproom: Wed to Fri, 4:30 to 8 p.m.; Sat, 12 to 7 p.m.

Life as a lawyer is quite different from life as a brewery owner. Porter Hardy can share his experiences firsthand; he gave up the former and opted for the latter when he "got tired of the lawyer gig" and realized that his homebrewing hobby was more than just a hobby; it was a passion that aligned with his dreams of starting his own business. Remember this when you try their delicious, refreshing **Alter Ego Saison**, named for "the alter ego in each of us."

Opening a 20-barrel brewhouse is no simple task, though, and fortunately Porter was joined by a group of friends and community members who all came together to invest in his concept for Smartmouth Brewing.

Based in Norfolk in an area that's been revitalized over recent years—on a commuting path between downtown and west Norfolk—the tasting room is now a place to congregate, to enjoy great beer among friends. The family-friendly tasting room is equipped with games and a chalkboard wall for kids (and sometimes adults) to doodle on, and in warm weather you can take your beer outside to the dog-friendly outdoor patio and deck. There are no televisions inside and long picnic tables are the main form of seating; it's designed that way—a communal space meant for socializing and chatting with your neighbor beside you.

There's no food served, but food trucks are frequently stationed outside, and there are a few local restaurants and pubs nearby where you can purchase food to bring along with you. Consider packing your own meat and cheese tray to bring

Alter Ego Saison
Style: Saison
ABV: 6.2%
Availability: Year-round on tap and in cans
Citrusy and a little spicy, this Belgian-style saison
is everything a saison should be. Crisp German
malts make up the backbone, the hops used give
it a sweet-smelling aroma, and its taste is overall
light bodied while also evoking peppery and lemony
flavors.

along, then get a pint of the **Notch 9 Double IPA**. At 9.1% ABV, its powerful flavor
will stand up to any strong cheese. For dessert, pack cookies or brownies and try
it with the **Cowcatcher Milk Stout**. Or just enjoy the stout on its own; its roasted
chocolate flavors and thick creamy head will make the perfect dessert.

ST. GEORGE BREWING
204 Challenger Way, Hampton, VA 23666; (757) 865-BEER; stgbeer.com;
@StGeorgeBrewery
Founded: 1996 **Founder:** Bill Spence **Brewers:** Andy Rathmann **Flagship Beer:**
English IPA **Year-Round Beers:** English IPA, Golden Ale, Porter, Pilsner, Nut Brown Ale
Seasonals/Special Releases: Spring Lager, Summer Ale, Winter Scotch, Oktoberfest
(see website for specifics) **Tours:** Mon to Fri, 3 p.m. **Taproom:** Mon to Fri, 3 to 5 p.m.;
Sat, 10 a.m. to 4 p.m.; retail shop: Mon to Fri, 8 a.m. to 5 p.m.

Established in 1996, this production brewery was one of the first Virginia breweries to open within coastal Virginia. What began as a brew-on-premise operation
in Virginia Beach moved to Hampton in 1999 and then to a larger location—their
current facility located in an industrial building on Challenger Way—as of the year
2000. Their 27-barrel brewhouse now distributes beer to places within Virginia,
Maryland, and North Carolina.

English IPA
Style: India Pale Ale
ABV: 5.5%
Availability: Year-round
Its deep amber color draws you in. This is a true English-style IPA made with 100% UK hops that give it a new kind of bitterness for those more familiar with American-style IPAs, while also being well balanced with its nice malt profile.

Painted in red, the tasting room is cozy with a few tables and a small bar, where you can sample their signature selection of beers like the **Golden Ale**, an old British recipe that uses American hops instead, or the **Porter**, also a more traditional English-style porter. During warm days you can take your beer out to the parking lot where there are occasionally food trucks.

YOUNG VETERANS BREWING COMPANY
2505 Horse Pasture Rd., Virginia Beach, VA 23453; (757) 689-4021; yvbc.com; @YoungVetsBrew
Founded: 2012 **Founders:** Thomas Wilder, Neil McCanon **Brewer:** Neil McCanon
Flagship Beers: New Recruit Honey Blonde Ale, Night Vision American Stout, Big Red Rye, Jet Noise Double IPA, Pineapple Grenade Hefeweizen **Year-Round Beers:** See flagships **Seasonals/Special Releases:** C4 India Brown Ale, Truce in the Forest, Goat Locker Breakfast Stout, Bravo Foxtrot (see website for more) **Tours:** Upon request
Taproom: Tues to Thurs, 3 to 10 p.m.; Fri, 3 to 11 p.m.; Sat, 12 to 11 p.m.; Sun, 3 to 8 p.m.

With a name like Young Veterans, it's obvious that founders Thomas Wilder and Neil McCanon's past military careers have had a significant influence on their lives, and if you're a military veteran yourself, you'll undoubtedly feel welcome at this cozy, friendly tasting room within an industrial area of Virginia Beach. There's even a long-standing military discount of 15% every day, all year round upon your visit.

Both Thomas and Neil share that life as a brewery owner gives them both independence as well as a full sense of responsibility, and they enjoy this aspect of running a business. It gives them the opportunity to support other causes as well, such as Vet Noise, monthly events that Young Veterans and the Hampton Roads Military Relocation Team host to support local veterans charities.

The military theme carries over to other aspects of their brewery business, too, like in their beer names. Try the **Pineapple Grenade**, a hefeweizen: the pineapple flavor is not overpowering; it's slightly camouflaged from what you might expect from its name—refreshing and subtly sweet. The light-bodied **New Recruit Honey Blonde Ale** or the more medium-bodied **Night Vision American Stout** are also usually available to sample. Other names include the **Semper FI.P.A**, the **Green Bullet**, and **C4 India Brown Ale**.

Sample these beers while you admire the flags and military memorabilia throughout the tasting room. You can also admire the copper art and jewelry inside, and even buy some if you so choose, because they share their space with friends and owners of a Copper Art Design gallery located in the building, friends who generously offered their space to Young Veterans Brewery and temporary free rent until Thomas and Neil got their business up and running.

To see the nanobrewery system, walk down a narrow entryway in back (past the bar) and on warm days, you can also walk through the brewery to a few outside picnic tables to enjoy your beer.

Beer Lover's Pick

Jet Noise
Style: Double IPA
ABV: 8%
Availability: Year-Round on tap and in cans
Loud and engulfing like its name—Jet Noise—this double IPA is heavily hopped and heavily engulfing in its bitterness, a must try for hopheads.

Brewpubs

HOME REPUBLIC

328 Laskin Rd., Virginia Beach, VA 23451; (757) 226-9593; www.homerepublic vabeach.com

Founded: 2014 **Founders:** Joe and Barbara Curtis **Brewer:** Joe Curtis **Flagship Beer:** King Kolsch, Galaxy IPA **Year-Round Beers:** King Kolsch, Galaxy IPA, Short & Stocky Stout **Seasonals/Special Releases:** Easy Rye Ale, Holiday Portly Stout, Juice Sea Fruit IPA

Home Republic is in a prime location, a one block walk to the beach, and near multiple Virginia beach hotels, which makes it an easy spot to stop for craft beer and a nice array of pub food. Not only that, but it's currently the *only* brewpub located in Virginia Beach.

The brewery part of the pub is at the back of the restaurant, a small nanobrewing operation where Joe Curtis, owner and homebrewer-turned-brewer, cranks out beers like their flagship **King Kolsch**, a light-bodied, easy-drinking beer at the beach, or some other more unusual combinations like the **Juice Sea Fruit IPA**, made with fresh oranges and grapefruit.

There are usually about 8 beers on draft. Unlike some brewpubs that will only serve their own brews on draft, Home Republic is mixing it up, by serving a few of their house specialties as well as other craft beer from breweries in Virginia and other parts of the US. Their small system allows them to constantly try different house brews to share with their customers. Since they opened in June 2014, they've put out over 150 different kinds of beer.

The typical food selections pair nicely with the beer—a nice burger menu, soups and salads, and entrees like beer-barbecued chicken and baby back ribs.

Since they don't serve liquor onsite, they've creatively added "beer tails and wine tails" to the menu, where you get concoctions like the Bloody IPA, a homemade Bloody Mary mix that uses IPA in place of vodka, or the Orange Shandy, made with sparkling orange juice and wheat beer.

Founder Joe Curtis served 20 years in the Marine Corps prior to starting his own business, and his goal is to make Home Republic a welcoming spot for both tourists and locals alike, a place where you can feel at home, whether your real home is in Virginia Beach or hundreds of miles away.

Beer Bars

THE BIRCH

**1231 W. Olney Rd., Norfolk, VA 23508; (757) 962-5400; thebirchbar.com;
Draft Beers:** 21 **Bottled/Canned Beers:** 80+

Craft beer bars are everywhere you look these days, but few have received the amount of recognition that The Birch has in its 4 short years since opening. For 3 years in a row (2012–2014), the bar was on RateBeer's List of the Top 50 Beer Bars (in the world!), as well as top beer bar lists on CraftBeer.Com and in *Draft* magazine. In 2013, it was even ranked the Number 3 Beer Bar in the entire US, according to ratebeer.com.

Beer snobs, beer geeks, and beer enthusiasts traveling through the coastal Virginia area will know to look for this place, but to others, at first glance it may seem an unlikely destination. Located in an industrial section of Norfolk, The Birch is in a revitalized neighborhood that now also is home to Smartmouth Brewing. It's simple and no-frills inside with an L-shaped bar, exposed HVAC system, and a garage door that opens to an outside seating area.

For food, it serves a selection of gourmet grilled cheese sandwiches, cheese and charcuterie boards, and bar snacks like cocktail nuts and popcorn. For beer, it has an ever-changing list of draft beers and specializes in hard-to-find rare beers. International beers are common, but they also usually carry a keg or two from selective Virginia breweries.

Mark your calendars for some of their special events. They do things slightly different than many beer bars that choose to host events like tap takeovers featuring just one select brewery. The Birch's events are "43 hours of" festivals; 43 hours meaning festivals that last 1 entire week (standing for the number of hours that The Birch bar is open every week). Usually these festivals feature select styles of beer, like 43 hours of bitter, 43 hours of sours, or 43 hours of dark.

A great way to test your palate and increase your craft beer expertise, but more importantly, sample an amazing selection of rare beer from the US and around the world—all in one unassuming spot in Norfolk.

DOG STREET PUB
401 W. Duke of Gloucester Street, Williamsburg, VA 23185; (757) 293-6478;
dogstreetpub.com
Draft Beers: 17 **Bottled/Canned Beers:** 130+

It's easy to be drawn to DoG Street Pub by its incredible location, along a shopping thoroughfare called Merchants Square—a brick-lined, quaint street filled with independent shops and close to all the major Colonial Williamsburg sights. It's just as easy to find too, especially once you know that its name is an acronym for its address—on the Duke of Gloucester Street.

Opened in 2012 by Chef David Everett, his vision, as general manager Michael Claar communicated, was to "convert an 80-year-old bank building with concepts from the flourishing gastropub movement and combine them with a menu of traditional pub food in a casual setting."

Heartwarming food is at the core of this; among the selections are fish and chips, roasted prime rib, and burger options—the traditional beef burger or a lamb burger, salmon burger, and even a brat burger. There are hearty small plates like Welsh rarebit (a cheesy plate of goodness) and Stout Chili (see In the Kitchen section for these recipes that you can try for yourself at home).

Chef Everett took it a step further when he hired Michael to create the beer program for the pub, and from there it's just continued to grow and develop. At the pub, you'll find a long bar to sit at (or opt for a table in the spacious dining area or outside to people-watch) with a large number of craft beer options—a rotating beer

list that showcases the local Virginia brews as well as import options, with 17 draft options including a cask ale. DoG Street Pub recently collaborated with Alewerks Brewing Company located just a few miles away to create an Extra Special Bitter style called Maizies, named after Chef Everett's Golden Doodle dog in the pub's logo.

After dining, walk outside around the corner where beer lovers will be wowed by the new addition to the DoG Street Pub business, their Hair of the Dog Bottle Shop, which houses another bar with 8 drafts, and walls and walls of beers, including three full shelves stocked with some great Virginia options. You'll also want to consider taking home a growler (62-ounce glass jug) full of beer or a Crowler (the newer 32-ounce portable aluminum can creation). If you've never seen a Crowler being filled, you'll want to sit at the bar at the bottle shop to get a front row view of the action.

Dive Bar with Amazing Craft Beer

LYNNHAVEN PUB
2236 W. Great Neck Rd., Virginia Beach, VA 23451; (757) 481-9720
Rave reviews from a number of Virginia Beach locals prompted a visit to this pub next to a shopping plaza on a side street. It almost went unnoticed. At first glance, it may appear the kind of dive bar that you would expect to walk into and be shunned if you didn't order a Bud Light.

Don't stereotype this place—just enter, have a seat at the bar, and be prepared to be wowed by the beer list. Order from the rotating draft menu, a large beer menu of over 140 bottles from around the US and Europe, and you can also get some nice house food selections like barbecue (pulled pork/brisket) and hearty sandwiches. If you're feeling cramped inside due to the narrow space, keep walking to the back where you'll find a pool table and a much larger tented outdoor space that's open throughout the year.

Southern & Southwest Virginia

Lots of wide-open country roads define this region. Small towns and church steeples dot the landscape. The breweries are spread out, and if you attempt to visit a few of them, you should also prepare for lots of time on the open road—great rural drives.

Some of the breweries in this chapter are just a few short miles from the state borders of Tennessee or North Carolina.

Many of the breweries in this region provide the great stuff that comes with life in a smaller town—a community atmosphere, a place to relax and hang out with friends and family, and occasional events hosted at the brewery to bring the community together.

THE BUSTED STILL BREWERY

185 Homeplace Dr., Gate City, VA 24251; (276) 386-6300
Founded: 2014 **Founders:** Rex and Lisa McCarty **Brewers:** Daniel Barnette, Jordan Peters **Flagship Beer:** Black Dog Stout **Year-Round Beers:** Boozy Creek Blonde, Patrick's Oatmeal Porter, Black Dog Stout, Allie O'Neil's Irish Red, Revenuers Imperial Amber **Seasonals/Special Releases:** Sir Hops A Lot Double IPA, Jennings Amber, Hoppy Toad IPA **Tours:** No **Taproom:** Wed and Thurs, 4 to 8 p.m.; Fri, 4 to 10 p.m.; Sat, 2 to 10 p.m.

It was always in the back of co-founder Rex McCarty's mind to own a bar, particularly one that would resemble an Irish pub. Maybe it was because of his Irish heritage, but it seemed like a pipe dream, until one night on a vacation to New Orleans he decided to begin turning that dream into a reality. Upon a trip to a brewery called

Crescent City, he and his wife began to price the cost of starting a nanobrewery back in their hometown in an old building on their historic farmstead—a place that, as referenced on the Virginia tourism website (virginia.org), houses a "collection of authentic structures and artifacts that have assembled here from their original locations throughout Scott County." Once a gift shop on the site of the farmstead, this building is now the pub and tasting room for the brewery.

The Busted Still Brewery has still only had a "soft opening," meaning people only find out about them through word of mouth or if they've liked them on their Facebook page, but that hasn't stopped hundreds of people finding out about this brewery and regularly filling up the spacious tasting room inside. There's a beer garden outside, and only one lone stone sign at the entrance advertising Busted Still Brewing. You have to know how to find this place.

They want to keep it that way for a while, mostly because their 1-barrel system limits the amount of beer they can produce. In the short time since their soft opening, they have experimented with a variety of styles while focusing on doing things in traditional, drinkable, and balanced flavors. That includes a **Boozy Creek Blonde**, a crisp refreshing blonde ale, and beers like the **Allie O'Neil's Irish Red**, to highlight their Irish roots. Bring your pets and your kids and hang out and settle in. That's the point. If you want to stay longer, you might even consider renting one of the cabins available on their farmstead, just a short walk down the hill from the brewery.

Beer Lover's Pick

Black Dog Stout
Style: Stout
ABV: 5.3%
Availability: Year-round on tap
Its deep black color and rich chocolate aromas will entice you to try this sweet-tasting, smooth-finishing beer. This is their flagship beer, and the beer that's most requested among their local community of followers.

CALLAWAY BREWING COMPANY

21 Woodwinds Rd., Callaway, VA 24067; (540) 267-6733; callawaybrewingco.com
Founded: 2013 **Founders:** Sterling White, Kevin Burroughs **Brewer:** Will Landry
Flagship Beers: Five Mile Mountain Amber Ale, Blackwater Porter **Year-Round Beers:**
Five Mile Mountain Amber Ale, Blackwater Porter, Freeborn IPA, White's Wheat **Seasonals/
Special Releases:** Woodsplitter Stout **Tours:** Upon request **Taproom:** Thurs, 6:30 to 8
p.m.; Fri, 6:30 to 9 p.m.; Sat, 2 to 9 p.m. (see Facebook or website for updates)

Sterling White, co-founder of Callaway Brewing, wasn't the first one in his family to get into homebrewing. His grandfather was a homebrewer, and his mom introduced him to it. Sterling's transformed homebrewing into a real nanobrewing operation today, with a 2-barrel brewing system in a garage on Woodwinds Road. Using local ingredients, Sterling describes that they're "working with local farmers aiming to build a brewery that offers authentic southwest VA products not found anywhere else."

They also hope to convert light beer drinkers—apparently there are quite a few in this area of southwest VA—"by spoiling their palates so they can't stand the taste of anything but craft beer."

Other Nanobreweries to Check Out in Southwest Virginia

2WITCHES WINERY & BREWING CO.

209 Trade St., Danville, VA 24541; 2witcheswinebrew.com
This brewery is a small family-owned winery and nanobrewery in Danville, where you'll often find up to six styles of beer at one time, including beer like the Hocus' Losin Focus, an 11.5% ABV Belgian quadrupel, as well as The Good Witch Blonde Ale and The Bad Witch Brown Ale, named for his daughter's homemade witch costumes that they wore many years ago for a photo.

OLD GLADE BREWERY

217 Town Sq., Glade Spring, VA 24340; oldgladebrewery.com
Founded by husband and wife team Tim and Rexanne, this brewery operation is small and a great community spot to check out during their tasting hours on Friday and Saturday evenings, where you can sample beers like their New River IPA, Copperhead IPA, Colonial Stout, and Amber Mountains Ale.

They might persuade these light drinkers by first letting them sample their **Five Mile Mountain Amber Ale** then their **White's Wheat Ale**, and maybe eventually persuade them to move on to their rich, toasted porter called the **Blackwater Porter**. Their taproom is currently open during limited time periods on Thursday and Friday evenings, and from 2 to 9 p.m. on Saturday, so be sure to confirm their schedule before you make the journey to Callaway to check out this niche nanobrewing operation.

THE DAMASCUS BREWERY

32173 Government Rd., Damascus, VA 24236; (540) 314-2782; thedamascusbrewery .com
Founded: 2013 **Founder:** Adam Woodson **Brewer:** Adam Woodson **Flagship Beer:** Beaver Rage IPA **Year-Round Beers:** Beaver Rage IPA, Backbone Bock, "OMG" Light **Seasonals/Special Releases:** Bazinga Black IPA, Beaver Fever Porter, Sweet Beaver Apricot Hefeweizen, Dankness Monster **Taproom:** Thurs and Fri, 6 to 9 p.m; Sat, 2 to 10 p.m.; Sun, 2 to 6 p.m.

The desire to move back to the Damascus area was how the idea for the brewery formed—and then solidified—for the Woodson family. Adam Woodson had a career in the chemical science industry sequencing DNA prior to transitioning to

Dankness Monster
Style: Imperial Red IPA
ABV: 9.75%
Availability: Rotating

The new favorite beer among the Damascus Brewery locals will creep up on you at 9.75% ABV. It's both hoppy and malty and has lots of great sweetness, but at the same time you'd never believe it was as high in alcohol as it is.

head brewer, owner, and any and all-other-encompassing roles (office administrator, janitor, welder) that come along with the day-to-day operation of a brewery.

As early as 2009, he started planning. An unfortunate company-wide massive layoff some time later (when he was living in Radford) gave him the stimulus he needed to make the move to Damascus and get the brewery set up.

Adam built the system himself, a 50-gallon nanobrewery assembled from stainless steel vats that were once used for dairy production. Consequently, it's a manual hands-on brewing cycle that often involves climbing ladders or step stools during parts of the brewing process to complete each batch.

While at the tasting room, you're also technically inside the brewhouse, so you can see the brewing system firsthand and get some understanding as to how it works. When you see how much manual labor was involved in getting it to its final stage, you might even agree that the already delicious beer that Adam brews tastes even better. The **Beaver Rage IPA** received rave reviews from the local Damascus crowd; one of their original flagships, it is packed with four different kinds of hops and finds its balance due to using those hops in later stages of the brewing process to achieve a great aroma and non-lingering bitterness. The malt lovers should try the **Backbone Bock** beer, a dark, malt-forward lager that tastes great any time of the year.

In warm weather, there are picnic tables outside and a cornhole game in place. In other times of the year, you can enjoy the interior space, where the wooden elements throughout make it cozy. There are dartboards and an L-shaped bar. Damascus Brewery's beaver mascot is evident, engraved into the bar, on the floor, and there's even a stuffed beaver on a shelf looking at you from above.

SUNKEN CITY BREWING COMPANY

40 Brewery Dr., Hardy, VA 24101; (540) 420-0476; sunkencitybeer.com; @SunkenCityBeer
Founded: 2012 **Founder:** Jerome Parnell **Brewers:** Jeremy Kirby, Seth Johnson
Flagship Beer: Dam Lager **Year-Round Beers:** Dam Lager, Red Clay IPA, Steemboat Beer **Seasonals/Special Releases:** Tartan Tent, Sunktoberfest, Crooked Road Cream Ale, Surfside Wheat, John Henry's Hammer Imperial Stout **Tours:** Private groups as scheduled, upon request (if staff is available) **Taproom:** Thurs and Fri, 3 to 9 p.m.; Sat, 12 to 9 p.m.; Sun, 12 to 5 p.m. (hours change seasonally, see website for specifics)

Sunken City Brewing is situated near Smith Mountain Lake in the town of Hardy, Virginia, a prime summer vacation zone, where tourists and Virginia residents flock to enjoy the outdoor activites along the 500 miles of shoreline and the 20,600-acre lake.

Beer Lover's Pick

Red Clay IPA
Style: India Pale Ale
ABV: 7.0%
Availability: Year-round
This beer is one of Sunken City's core offerings and is distributed in cans throughout many parts of Virginia and North Carolina. Piney and citrus notes prevail in the hop profile, but it's not over the top. You can still taste some of its sweet, malty attributes, resulting in a delicate balance of flavors.

Named for an actual Sunken City—the village that was flooded when the lake was dammed back in the 1960s—this brewery is a large 8,800-square-foot brewhouse, tasting room, and beer garden. It's part of the Westlake Town Center commercial complex, which includes local businesses, restaurants, shops, and a movie theater. When you enter the plaza, it will not be difficult to find Sunken City Brewing. It stands alone on its own street, Brewery Drive, within the Town Center complex.

The tasting room is modern, painted in green with dark wood tables and a bar. Snacks and chips are available inside; during the warmer months food trucks frequently park outside.

Your eyes will be drawn to a large mural covering one wall with a map of the area, marking the spot of the sunken city and portraying its history, which you can read and observe in more detail while you sip on one of their flagships, like the **Dam Lager**, an amber-colored refreshing choice on a summer day at the lake. As summer turns to fall, you might want to look out for their seasonal offerings, like the **Sunktoberfest**, a Märzen-style beer or in colder months, the **Tartan Tent**, a Scottish-style export ale with caramel undertones.

WOLF HILLS BREWING COMPANY
350 Park St., Abingdon, VA 24210; (276) 451-5470; wolfhillsbrewing.com; @WolfHills
Founded: 2009 **Founders:** Cameron Bell, Rich Buddington, Chris Burcher, Matt Bundy **Brewer:** Drake Scott **Flagship Beer:** White Blaze Honey Cream Ale, Troopers Alley IPA **Year-Round Beers:** White Blaze Honey Cream Ale, Troopers Alley IPA, Creeper Trail Amber Ale, Wolf Den Double IPA, Fightin' Parson's Pale Ale **Seasonals/Special Releases:** Chocolate Milk Stout, Oktoberfest, Pumpkin Porter, White IPA, Watermelon Wheat, Limited Release Barrel-Aged Beers **Tours:** No **Taproom:** Tues to Fri, 5 to 8 p.m.; Sat, 1 to 8 p.m. (hours change seasonally, see website for specifics)

Music and beer are often the themes at this old icehouse transformed into an all-in-one brewery, stage, and tasting room in the town of Abingdon. Wolf Hills Brewing has had their headquarters here since 2010 after moving from a 200-square-foot facility in 2009. They not only greatly increased the space they have, but they also increased their brew system, from their beginning setup on a 1-barrel system to today's 7-barrel system with 7-, 15-, and 30-barrel fermenters.

Those fermenters are constantly filled with some of their great flagship beers like the **White Blaze Honey Cream Ale**, a light ale that's smooth with a touch of sweetness (there's pure Appalachian honey used in this recipe). Another signature beer is the **Troopers Alley IPA**, a hop-forward IPA with lots of citrus and bitterness. They named this beer after a local point of interest, a side street once named Troopers Alley, where "men could find dens of evil fame, gambling, and strong ale" according to the brewery website.

Fewer than 10,000 people currently live in the small town of Abingdon, but residents are fortunate to have a place to go where they can drink local beer (average of 12 to 14 beers on tap) and attend some fun events, like open mike nights, trivia nights, and occasional special events tastings in an upstairs private event room. In addition to the regular bands they line up to perform at the brewery, the Wolf Hills

Wolf Den Double IPA
Style: India Pale Ale
ABV: 9.5%
Availability: Seasonal
When the IBU (bitterness ratio) reaches 100, you know you're in for a truly hoppy beer. Wolf Den achieves this with a plentiful amount of English hops and an American pale ale malt bill.

team is getting ready to host their own music festivals at remote locations in future years. They've often attracted some bigger shows inside the brewery, where hundreds of people buy tickets to attend. The space allows for this—garage doors that open up to create an open air atmosphere during the warmer months and a huge warehouse space that can easily function as a big event venue and as a hang-out spot for fresh local craft beer.

Brewpubs

BULL & BONES BREWHAUS & GRILL

1470 S. Main St., Suite 120, Blacksburg, VA 24060; (540) 953-BULL (2855);
bullandbones.com
Founded: 2008 **Founders:** Mark Shrader, Jon Coburn **Brewer:** Jim Strickland **Flagship Beers:** All Night Lite, The Lunch Pale Ale, Maroon Effect Ale, Strick's IPA, St. Maeve's Stout, Sun Lit Wit **Year-Round Beers:** Same as flagships **Seasonals/Special Releases:** Summer Hefe

Bull & Bones Brewhaus has a classic all-American sports bar atmosphere with the added bonus of billiard tables and fresh beer made onsite. The bar is long and narrow, with plenty of stools and an opportunity to watch your sport of choice on the HDTVs lined up in front of you. Look behind the TVs and the bar to get a glimpse of the 10-barrel brew system where beers like the **Maroon Effect Ale**, a malty caramel brown ale, or the **St. Maeve's Stout**, a rich but dry Irish stout, will pair well with your meat of choice.

Bull selections on the menu include steaks like sirloin, beef rib-eye, and filet, while a *bone* selection could mean house pork ribs, pulled pork, or beef brisket. There are also plenty of other options that fit in the No Bones About It menu category—something for everyone. If your dinner party includes some in the under-21 crowd,

there's a casual dining area separated from the bar, cocktail tables, and billiards area to enjoy a quieter dinner and atmosphere.

RIVER COMPANY RESTAURANT AND BREWERY

6633 Viscoe Rd., Fairlawn, VA 24141; (540) 633-3940; therivercompanyrestaurant .com;
Founded: 2008 **Founder:** Mark Hall, Barbara and John Hall, Mary Beth Greer **Brewer:** Mike Pensinger **Flagship Beer:** Farmhouse Hefeweizen **Year-Round Beers:** Fairlawn's Finest Cream Lager, River Red Ale, Timber Brown Ale, Farmhouse Hefeweizen, Traveler's Pale Ale, Southwest "V" India Pale Ale, Dumpster Dog Porter **Seasonals/Special Releases:** Peachicot Blonde Ale (plus many more experimental and seasonal offerings frequently on tap at the brewpub—call for specifics)

The River Company Restaurant fulfills many roles for the Fairlawn community. It's a state of the art restaurant, a place for students to celebrate with their families after getting their degree at one of the nearby colleges like Radford University or New River Community College, and often even a wedding venue that has a separate

private event room. Above all, especially for readers of this book, it's a brewpub, soon to be more of a brewery than a brewpub as they focus on rebranding themselves and dedicate more of their time to distribution.

This brewpub offers customers 8 year-round beer selections including beer like the **Farmhouse Hefeweizen** and **Timber Brown Ale.** Most of their regular offerings are considered session oriented at around 6% ABV or less.

In addition to all the regulars, Mike Pensinger, who's been chief brewer for the River Company throughout most of its existence, often brews some experimental and new recipes of his own. Recent limited-batch varieties have included some delicious options like the **Chile Chaser Spiced Stout** and a stronger, hoppier beer called the **Shot Tower Imperial IPA.** Mike's had a long background in the brewing industry. From homebrewing to owning a homebrew shop—one that's now grown into being a large, successful homebrew shop in the US called Homebrew USA (see BYOB: Brew Your Own Beer section)—to working and developing the beer reputation at a brewery in coastal Virginia, Mike knows his stuff.

Mike fortunately has a nice brewery to work from too, based downstairs at the River Company. From the bar, you can see partially into the 10-barrel brewery downstairs through glass windows. In the brewery, there are high ceilings and some great space to move around, not always common in other breweries and brewpubs I've seen.

The brewery space is by itself a well-built, well-designed space, but what's even more impressive is the main restaurant and bar area on the first floor. It's a wide-open, spacious, and tall room built in traditional timber frame construction, each joint hand cut and crafted by craftsmen from Lancaster, Pennsylvania. Large doors open up to outside tables where you can admire the scenic views overlooking the country and nearby towns. Sit down and take in the scene as you enjoy the beer and food made from scratch. The meat is dry-aged in house. Mike shares that this place was envisaged as a destination. It seems to have accomplished that.

Multilocation Brewpubs & Beer Bars

Multilocation brewpubs and beer bars throughout the state's various regions are highlighted in this chapter.

Before you brush them aside because of their status as a "chain" brewpub or beer bar, check out what they have to offer. In certain cases, though they're part of a bigger corporation, they're still helping to increase people's exposure to craft beer within their town or region, and each location may be doing something unique; individual brewmasters at the multilocation brewpubs often have some freedom to make alterations and create new recipes. Multilocation beer bars often have the ability to get one-off kegs to support their local or regional community and small beer businesses.

Brewpubs

EXTRA BILLY'S SMOKEHOUSE

Midlothian, 1110 Alverser Dr., Midlothian, VA 23113; (804) 379-8727
Richmond, 5205 W. Broad St., Richmond, VA 23230; (804) 282-9349
extrabillys.com
Founded: 1996 **Founders:** Robert and Judy Harr **Brewmaster:** Dylan Brooks **Beers:**
Extra Billy's Brown Ale, Midlo Pale Ale, El Jefe, Hoptrick, Kong Krus, Citra Ass Down, My
Only Weiss, ForeCzech Pilsner (see Facebook page for more specifics or call)

Barbecue and beer just go together, and Extra Billy's was one of the earlier established brewpubs in the Richmond vicinity that figured out that this would make a smart business model. They have two locations in the Richmond surrounding area, but all the beer is brewed at the Midlothian location, where head brewer Dylan Brooks is in charge of the brewing operation.

Barbecue favorites like beef brisket, baby back ribs, and Texas-smoked sausage are served up alongside some equally bold, tasty beer like the **Extra Billy's Brown Ale**, a deep brown medium-bodied ale, or the **Citra Ass Down**, an IPA packed with Citra hops.

GORDON BIERSCH BREWERY RESTAURANT

McLean, 7861 Tysons Corner Center, McLean, VA 22102; (703) 388-5454
Virginia Beach, 4561 Virginia Beach Blvd., Virginia Beach, VA 23462;
(757) 490-2739
gordonbiersch.com
Founded: 1998 **Founders:** Dan Gordon, Dean Biersch **Brewmaster:** Dan Gordon
(director of brewing operations); each location has its own brewmaster: Justin Damadio
(McLean), Eddie Leal (Virginia Beach) **Year-Round Beers:** Märzen, Golden Export,
HefeWeizen, Pilsner **Seasonals/Special Releases:** Winterbock, Festbier, Maibock,
Blonde Bock, Summerbrau (see website for each specific location for more info)

Gordon Biersch has a long history synonymous with great beer, with a focus on German-style beers. The Gordon Biersch Brewery opened in San Jose, California, in 1997, and the first brewery restaurant opened in 1998 in Palo Alto, California. Today, there are more than 30 locations throughout the US.

In Northern Virginia, the Gordon Biersch McLean location is based at one of the largest shoping malls in the DC area, Tyson's Corner, which at first glance is not

exactly the most picturesque spot. Still, it's proved to be successful, a great escape from the flurry of people in a shopping frenzy. The space inside can make you forget that you're in a mall, especially once you grab a table at the 436-seat restaurant and look to the back of the room where you can see the 10-barrel brewing system behind a glass wall, and maybe even watch the brewmaster of this location, Justin

Damadio, in action, while munching on their signature Garlic Fries.

Justin is regularly brewing beers like the **Märzen**, described as "an auburn colored Bavarian lager with a mildly sweet, Munich malt finish" and the **Hefeweizen**, a traditional German wheat beer. Yet he is also getting the chance to contribute his own recipes, as are the other brewmasters across the Gordon Biersch locations. The Scottish Ale he brewed in the fall of 2014 is a good example; he used a Wee Heavy, Scottish Ale and a Scotch Ale recipe and melded them all together. Justin explained it as "taking something out of every little bit of my brewing history and combining it into one beer."

Gordon Biersch is investing in some highly experienced brewers who are all bringing something unique to the table, while also sticking with what they've become known for in their German-style beers and signature lagers.

ROCK BOTTOM BREWERY

Arlington, 4238 Wilson Blvd., Suite 1256, Arlington, VA 22203; (703) 516-7688
Richmond Short Pump, 11800 W. Broad St., Richmond, VA 23233; (804) 237-1684
rockbottom.com
Founded: 1991 **Founder:** Frank Day **Brewmaster:** Each location has its own
brewmaster. Richmond location—Becky Hammond, Arlington location—Chris Jacques
Year-Round Beers: Kölsch, White Ale, IPA, Red Ale, Special Dark **Seasonals/Special
Releases:** Rocktoberfest, Cask-Conditioned Ales, Brewmaster's Choice

Denver, Colorado, was the site of the first Rock Bottom Brewery Restaurant in 1991, and though that was the original, today there are over 30 Rock Bottom Restaurants across the US. In 2010 it was sold to Craftworks Restaurants & Breweries Inc., a multi-brand restaurant operator that also owns the Gordon Biersch brewpubs and another casual pizza joint with multiple locations named Old Chicago.

There are two locations in Virginia. The Richmond location is in the Short Pump Town Center, a shopping plaza northwest of downtown Richmond, while the Arlington location is in the Ballston Common mall in Northern Virginia, a four-level shopping plaza. Both are prime locations in busy areas of Virginia.

The Arlington location is near some large business offices and hotels, making it a great spot to visit after a long, hard day in the office. Once inside the Rock Bottom in Arlington, you'll forget you're in a mall. The interior has a nice-sized bar and

cocktail area when you enter and the brewing equipment is behind the bar through glass windows. There's also a large restaurant seating area inside, painted in warm colors of reds and mustard yellow with lots of wood fixtures throughout.

All locations have a signature beer lineup that you can always rely on, like the **Kölsch**, a light-bodied golden, crisp ale, and the **White Ale**, a slightly hazy ale with citrus notes from its orange peel essence you can smell and taste.

Though each location will have similarities, like made-from-scratch food and a casual overall atmosphere and feel, the brewmasters have some freedom to create their own innovative beer recipes as well (the number of taps they have to put on their own beer will vary at each location), and so each Rock Bottom location will offer some unique beer that you can't get at other locations. Be sure to ask about these selections during your visit.

SWEETWATER TAVERN

Centreville, 14250 Sweetwater Ln., Centreville, VA 20121; (703) 449-1100
Merrifield, 3066 Gate House Plaza, Falls Church, VA 22042; (703) 645-8100
Sterling, 45980 Waterview Plaza, Sterling, VA 20166; (571) 434-6500
greatamericanrestaurants.com
Founded: 2000 **Founders:** Randy Norton, Mike Ranney, Jim Farley **Brewmaster:** Joe Schineller **Year-Round Beers:** Great American Resturants Pale Ale, Naked River Light **Seasonals/Special Releases:** Crazy Jackass Ale, Great American Restaurants Octoberfest, Yippe Ei O Springbock, High Desert Imperial Stout (see website for more)

Multiple location brewpubs are often connected with the less positive association of "chain restaurant," making certain beer enthusiasts turn into skeptics about the beer's quality and the types of beers they make.

Here's a challenge for any of you skeptics out there: Visit any of the three Sweetwater Tavern locations in Northern Virginia. Go in with an open mind, try the beer, sit at the bar and admire the southwest decor around you. You're highly likely to forget about all that original skepticism and become a believer.

Sweetwater Tavern has two year-round beers and over 35 different seasonal recipes that they rotate throughout the year, providing a pleasing variety to any craft beer lover. Head brewmaster Joe Schineller along with brewers Jake Sullivan and Steve Babler are responsible for creating and maintaining those recipes, as well as inventing, tweaking, and examining other new and old recipes throughout the year. Expect 5 beers on tap at each location.

In the brewery, they use counter-pressure growler fillers to keep the beer fresh and delicious, extending the shelf life of the growler from what's normally a range

of about 7 to 14 days maximum to upwards of 90 days. A silo filled with German pilsner malt is a rarity at most brewpubs, but Sweetwater Tavern has it, and uses all that great malt to create the base flavor in many of their best beer recipes—recipes that have won them a number of awards at the Great American Beer Festival in recent years. One of those winners was their flagship beer, the **Great American Restaurants Pale Ale**, a copper-colored ESB-style ale that uses a Whitbread Golding hop variety from the UK to achieve the perfect balance of bitter and sweet. Other great offerings include a **Sidewinder Bock** beer, a German-style doppelbock that is a nice choice for those who love the strong and malty flavors. Try an assertive, full-flavored beer like their **High Desert Imperial Stout** that resonates with dominant notes of rich chocolate.

Drink your beer in spacious, comfy surroundings, understanding that you're at one of the restaurants owned by the Great American Restaurants Group, a successful corporation that runs and operates a dozen restaurants in the Northern Virginia region with a mission to be the "World's Best Operator of Casual Restaurants."

Every Sweetwater Tavern restaurant evokes an Old West theme, from the hand-made rugs that were purchased in Sante Fe, New Mexico, to the hand-painted murals covering the walls (painted by John Gable) at each location. Pair your beer with the Drunken Rib Eye steak, marinated in the Great American Restaurants Pale Ale beer, to complete your night.

Beer Bars

CAPITAL ALE HOUSE

Fredericksburg, 917 Caroline St., Fredericksburg, VA 22401; (804) 780-ALES
Harrisonburg, 41-A Court Sq., Harrisonburg, VA 22801; (540) 564-ALES
Innsbrook, 4024-A Cox Rd., Glen Allen, VA 23060; (804) 780-ALES
Richmond, 623 E. Main St., Richmond, VA 23219; (804) 780-ALES
Midlothian, 1381 Village Place Dr., Midlothian, VA 23114; (804) 780-ALES
capitalalehouse.com
Draft Beers: 60 **Bottled/Canned Beers:** 250+

The original Capital Ale House location in Richmond opened in 2002. When it opened it was one of the few craft beer spots in town, a huge risk at the time for the owners who took a chance on their niche craft beer–focused bar and gutted out a very old building in downtown Richmond. It paid off!

Today, there are four other Capital Ale House locations, and you'll no doubt know of its strong reputation if you're one of the beer geeks in the Richmond community or throughout Virginia.

In addition to other events, the Capital Ale House sponsors the National Beer Expo (nationalbeerexpo.com) that's held in Richmond on an annual basis, when many breweries around the country gather to showcase great American craft beer.

Capital Alehouse proudly promotes the Virginia beer scene in its many draft and bottled selections, and has an extensive food menu that pairs great with the extraordinary beer menu.

JACK BROWN'S BEER AND BURGER JOINT

Charlottesville, 109 Second St. SE, Charlottesville, VA 22902; (434) 244-0073
Elkton, 11702 Spotswood Tr., Elkton, VA 22827; (540) 289-5092
Harrisonburg, 80 S. Main St., Harrisonburg, VA 22801; (540) 433-5225
Richmond, 5810 Grove Ave., Richmond, VA 23226; (804) 285-1758
Roanoke, 210B Market St. SE, Roanoke, VA 24011; (540) 342-0328
jackbrownsjoint.com
Draft Beers: each location differs **Bottled/Canned Beers:** 100+

Established in Harrisonburg by two best friends, Aaron Ludwig and Mike Sabin, this bar is exactly what its name says—a beer and burger joint. It can get crowded, so if you're one of the lucky ones to grab a seat inside the place, you'll want to claim that seat as long as you can. You'll have many jealous onlookers!

It's a fun, lively dive bar atmosphere, with decorations like bras and disco balls to complete the theme—a classic American joint.

Each location offers something unique to its local region. The Richmond location featured a tap takeover and an incredible live band only a few short weeks after the location opened to the public.

MELLOW MUSHROOM

Blacksburg, 207 S. Main St., Blacksburg, VA 24060; (540) 605-7074
Bristol, 3500 Lee Hwy., Bristol, VA 24201; (276) 644-3663
Charlottesville, 1321 W. Main St., Charlottesville, VA 22903; (434) 972-9366
Herndon, 1030 Elden St., Herndon, VA 20170; (703) 707-9300
Newport News, 12090 Jefferson Ave., Suite 1500, Newport News, VA 23602; Phone TBD (coming soon)
Richmond, 3012 W. Cary St., Richmond, VA 23221; (804) 370-8210
mellowmushroom.com
Draft Beers: see individual location **Bottled/Canned Beers:** see individual location to confirm

Established in 1974 in the state of Georgia, Mellow Mushroom now has over 150 locations throughout the US, and six in Virginia alone. Their mission is clear cut and simple, "to provide delicious food in a fun and creative environment."

That environment began with their Mellow Pies, tasty gourmet pizzas, and today has extended into a large selection of craft beer, lots of local stuff as well as international stuff.

Join the beer club to track your beer and have the option for rewards along the way. The casual, mellow and laid-back atmosphere will await you at every location, but the beer selections will differ slightly, focusing on their plan to work with as many local breweries as possible to help spread the word.

WORLD OF BEER

Arlington, 901 N. Glebe Rd., #105, Arlington, VA 22203
Charlottesville, 852 W. Main St., Charlottesville, VA 22903
Reston, 1888 Explorer St., Reston, VA 20190
worldofbeer.com
Draft Beers: 50 **Bottled/Canned Beers:** 500

There's no doubt with a name like World of Beer that their focus is the beer. It shows when you speak to the staff at any of the World of Beer locations. At the Northern Virginia location on Glebe Road, I tested the staff's beer knowledge, and they passed with flying colors.

Like any franchised location, it has its regular beers and regular distribution relationships, but what I also like is that, at least in the Northern Virginia location, they devote quite a few of their taps to Virginia beers—including half a refrigerator to various Virginia microbrew bottles. So in addition to the whole world of beer, you can also experience the world of Virginia beer.

Multilocation Craft Beer–Focused Restaurants

AMERICAN TAP ROOM
americantaproom.com

American Tap Room restaurants strive to "redefine the idea of casual sophistication . . . offering an outstanding selection of the finest food quality and service at an affordable price," as Maggie Nunn, director of marketing, shares with me. Craft beer is a large focus at all of their locations, where they offer a selection of craft beer from around the country but also feature some local breweries as well. Reston was their first Virginia location, opening in 2008. Since then they've expanded into Clarendon and Richmond. Expect anywhere from 25 to 50 beers on tap and 40+ bottle offerings.

DOGFISH HEAD ALEHOUSE
dogfishalehouse.com

It's not often that you get the opportunity to drink 18 different kinds of Dogfish Head beers on draft unless you're near where it is all brewed at the Dogfish Head Brewery in Milton, Delaware, or at their original brewpub in Rehoboth Beach.

Fortunately, Northern Virginia residents have their pick of two locations that offer direct access to those beers. There are three Dogfish Head Alehouses within the US, all the result of licensing agreements made in previous years, one in Gaithersburg, Maryland, one in Fairfax, Virginia, and another in Falls Church, Virginia. At the Alehouses, you can expect to find a great selection of hearty pub food and wood-fired pizzas and sandwiches. Try the interesting menu items made with beer, like the IPA Grouper Sandwich or the Raison d'Etre Infused Bratwurst.

From the outside, the Dogfish locations are easy to miss. Both locations are in the middle of shopping center complexes. Once you get inside, you'll be glad you made a point to find it. Just remember to have a designated driver with all the amazing beer selections with above-average ABV levels, from the more well-known Dogfish Head 60 (6% ABV) and 90 minute IPAs (9% ABV), to special releases like the Old School Barleywine, in the 13 to 16% ABV range.

FIREWORKS PIZZA

fireworkspizza.com

Fireworks Pizza operates two locations, one in Arlington and one in Leesburg, focusing on wood-fired pizzas, salads, and sandwiches. What's particularly impressive is that during a visit to the Arlington location, there were over 100 bottled beer varieties and over 30 beers on tap. Old Ox Brewery, Hardywood, Port City Brewing, and Mad Fox were among the breweries represented in Virginia at the time of my visit, but that's constantly rotating.

HEAVY SEAS ALEHOUSE

heavyseasalehouse.com

An affiliate of the Heavy Seas Brewery based in Baltimore, Maryland, this beer bar and restaurant is one of two Heavy Seas Alehouse locations, but the only one in Virginia. Their Arlington location is strategically located near big office complexes, hotels, and residential apartment buildings, as well as just a short 2 miles from major Washington, DC, sites such as the Washington Monument and the Lincoln Memorial.

Famous for their Loose Cannon beer, an American IPA packed with five different kinds of hops, Heavy Seas now has a multitude of beer options available. About half of the 15 taps allow you to try the Heavy Seas specialties, while the other half are designated for other local Virginia craft beer selections. Food selections incorporate some great Maryland-based food like crab cakes while you take in the atmosphere complete with a nautical-inspired theme, including reclaimed buoys and a mural of the Baltimore harbor from the 1920s.

RUSTICO RESTAURANT

rusticorestaurant.com

With a mission to "deliver a one two punch of honest cooking against a backdrop of amazing beer," the Rustico restaurants in Alexandria and Arlington attract large, local followers with their supply of over 400 beers. Rotating draft selections pair with their menu items like pizzas, burgers, entrees like filet and monkfish, and mussel starters.

SEDONA TAPHOUSE

sedonataphouse.com

Step inside the Sedona Taphouse in Midlothian and you immediately are drawn to the area behind the long bar, where you notice an attractive brick wall facade and rustic brown colors next to side-by-side beer refrigerators and 50 draft beer taps. Sedona Taphouse has locations in both Midlothian and Charlottesville in Central Virginia.

Beer Festivals

Taking a road trip around Virginia may not be something you can easily arrange to do. Don't worry, there's a viable backup option: beer festivals. Here, you can often sample many of the fresh microbrewed beer varieties available in Virginia, as well as gain some insight into the beer scene around the rest of the US.

Below is a sampling of some recurring festivals, though by no means a comprehensive list. Please note that many breweries now host their own festivals onsite or in their home regions that may or may not be listed here, so check out your local brewery's website or social media pages to stay up to date on all the ongoing events.

January

FREDERICKSBURG FROSTY BREW THRU
Fredericksburg Fairgrounds, 2400 Airport Ave., Fredericksburg, VA 22401; frostybrewthru.com

This indoor festival in the middle of January is the perfect way to get out of the house in the dead of winter. 2015's festival featured an East vs. West event with eight breweries from the West and eight from the East. It was a 7-hour event held over a Saturday afternoon.

February

MAD FOX BARLEYWINE FESTIVAL
Mad Fox Brewing Company, 444 W. Broad St., Falls Church, VA, 22046; madfoxbrewing.com

Every year, Northern Virginia residents should mark their calendars for this annual barleywine festival held at Mad Fox Brewing over the course of 2 days, where there will be on average 16 to 17 top barleywines from various breweries around the US to try.

Note: Mad Fox Brewing holds many great festivals throughout the year, including a Strong Beer tasting in March, a Spring Bock Festival, a Hoppy Oktoberfest, and a Cask Ale Festival. Be sure to check out their website for all of their events.

April

ROCKTOWN BEER AND MUSIC FESTIVAL
Turner Pavilion, 228 S. Liberty St., Harrisonburg, VA 22801; rocktownfestival.com
Hosted by the Harrisonburg Downtown Renaissance Community, this festival is usually held twice a year, once in the spring and in the fall, at the Turner Pavilion (the Farmer's Market Pavilion for those familiar with the Harrisonburg area). The festival hopes to show off America's craft beer culture, where "each brewery is handpicked and will be represented at the festival by a member of that brewery." Recent festivals have included an offering of 60+ craft beers with over 30 craft breweries represented, as well as a variety of bands and regular live music.

May

VIRGINIA BEER FESTIVAL
Town Point Park, Waterside Drive, Norfolk, VA 23510; vafest.org
Part of the Virginia Arts Festival, and co-presented with Festevents, this is a 2-day festival. According to the festival website, "Named one of the best beer festivals by *USA Today* (2013), this event takes place in Town Point Park on the beautiful downtown Norfolk waterfront featuring 65 breweries with more than 125 beers to sample."

June

HOPS AND HOWLERS CRAFT BREW FEST
Remsburg Drive, Abingdon, VA, 24210; hopsandhowlers.com
A newer festival organized in historic downtown Abingdon, this festival features beer from over 25 regional microbreweries and music all day long.

August

DOG STREET PUB CRAFT BEER FESTIVAL,
Merchants Square, 401 W. Duke of Gloucester St., Williamsburg, VA 23185; dogstreetpub.com
Known as one of the largest beer festivals on the peninsula, this festival offers all you can eat and all you can drink for the price of your admission fee. It's based outside among the Merchants Square shopping district in scenic Colonial Williamsburg and features many Virginia-based breweries.

MICROFESTIVUS
Elmwood Park, Jefferson Street, Roanoke, VA 24011; microfestivus.square
society.org

This 6-hour-long August festival is almost 20 years old and with your purchase, you can get either ten 4-ounce beer tastings or twenty 4-ounce beer tastings from breweries like Devils Backbone, Wild Wolf Brewing, Starr Hill Brewing, Stone Brewing, and Troegs Brewing. A great way to explore some Virginia breweries as well as sample the offerings from other states throughout the US at a beautiful park in Roanoke.

VIRGINIA CRAFT BREWERS FEST
Devils Backbone Basecamp Brewpub, 200 Mosbys Run, Roseland, VA 22967;
vacraftbrewersfest.com

Thousands of people travel to the base of the Blue Ridge Mountains to attend this beer festival that's held at Devils Backbone Basecamp Brewpub. Try beer from over 50 breweries throughout Virginia and when you get hungry, order your food from the Central Virginia food trucks that set up during the event. Enjoy the scenery and stay for the night after you attend the festival—camping and overnight spaces are available for tents or RVs. This festival is also the time when all the breweries compete for a chance to win a medal in the Virginia Beer Cup.

September

LYNCHBURG WINE AND BEER FESTIVAL
Lynchburg City Stadium, 3176 Fort Ave., Lynchburg, VA 24501;
lynchburgbeerandwinefestival.com

Originating in 2010, this festival continues to grow. Last year there were over 5,000 guests. This 8-hour festival includes with your ticket price (between $20 and $25 dependent upon whether you purchase your ticket at the gate or in advance) unlimited wine samples and ten 3-ounce beer samples. Beer includes approximately 100 different varieties from breweries both in Virginia and outside of Virginia. There are a variety of food tents, and live music at certain times of the day.

ROCKTOWN BEER AND MUSIC FESTIVAL
Turner Pavilion, 228 S. Liberty St., Harrisonburg, VA 22801; rocktownfestival.com
See description above, under month of April.

TOP OF THE HOPS BEER FEST

Telos Wireless Pavilion, 700 E. Main St., Charlottesville, VA 22902; topofthehopsbeerfest.com

Starr Hill Brewery and Beer Run are the presenting sponsors of this annual festival in Charlottesville, a beer-tasting experience that showcases over 150 beers from Virginia and other parts of the world—mostly other US breweries—but in past years there have been international brands like Duvel too. In addition to music and games, there have often been beer education sessions in past years, like a beer tasting class and a food and beer pairing class.

October

MID-ATLANTIC OKTOBERFEST

Capitol City Brewing Company, The Village at Shirlington, 4001 Campbell Ave., Arlington, VA 22206; (703) 578-3888; capcitybrew.com

Hosted by Capitol City Brewing Company, this annual festival has become bigger and bigger in recent years, now promoting itself as the "largest Oktoberfest beer festival in Northern Virginia." Streets are closed off throughout Shirlington Village during the festival, and in recent years there were more than 60 breweries that participated, along with local food vendors, German bands, and plenty of great Oktoberfest food like wursts and pretzels.

THE FESTY EXPERIENCE

Devils Backbone Basecamp Brewpub, 200 Mosbys Run, Roseland, VA 22967; thefesty.com

Founded in 2009 by co-creators Justin Billcheck and Michael Allenby, this annual festival every October takes place over the course of 3 days on the Devils Backbone grounds. Festival attendees can pick and choose the type of experience they want, including camping onsite that ranges from parking your own RV and setting up your own tent, to purchasing an upgrade where you can arrive to full tents already set up for you, to solid ground shelters (spacious 17-foot-diameter cotton-canvas tents) that have pillows and bedding. Events throughout the 3-day festival include some fabulous live music and activities like races, daily yoga, and kids' activities like a climbing wall and arts and crafts workshops. All this goes on while you enjoy incredible Blue Ridge Mountains views and Devils Backbone beer!

November

AUTUMN BOTTOM BREWS FESTIVAL

17th Street Farmers Market, 100 N. 17th St., Richmond, VA 23219; (804) 646-0954; enrichmond.org

This festival showcases Virginia beer from over 15 regional breweries, along with local food and live music. A great Sunday afternoon event in November.

Beer Bus Tours
& Self-Guided Trails

If you're still finding it difficult to decide where to start your beer journey, or you know where you want to go but don't want to worry that you'll be stuck in the role of designated driver, you'll be happy to know that many companies and organizations have services that will accommodate your beer-drinking and beer sightseeing plans.

BLUE RIDGE BEERWAY, visitroanokeva.com/things-to-do/breweries/blueridgebeer loop

In the spirit of offering craft beer fans an opportunity to complete their own self-guided beer trail, Virginia's Roanoke area and Blue Ridge Mountain region have launched the Blue Ridge Beerway, often called the Blue Ridge Beer Loop. It includes a do-on-your-own tour of eight different breweries. North of Roanoke, there are breweries like Flying Mouse Brewery in Troutsville and Parkway Brewing in Salem, while the beerway extends as far south as Callaway Brewing in Callaway.

BREW RIDGE TRAIL, brewridgetrail.com

This self-guided route gives you a map and a sample itinerary for your beer trip around Nelson and Albemarle Counties, as well as to downtown Charlottesville. Many of the same breweries that you'll find on the Nelson 151 trail below are included, as well as other nearby spots in close driving proximity, like Starr Hill Brewery, one of the oldest craft breweries in this part of Virginia, and South Street Brewery, a cozy brewpub in downtown Charlottesville.

NELSON 151, nelson151.com

Route 151 is a byway next to the Blue Ridge Mountains, but it's way more than just a scenic drive. Nelson 151 is now a "travel destination for Virginia wine, craft beer, hard cider, spirits and outdoor recreation lovers," according to its website. This self-guided trail includes seven wineries, three beer destinations (Devils Backbone

Basecamp Brewpub, Wild Wolf Brewing Company, and Blue Mountain Brewery), a cidery, and a distillery.

RICHMOND BREWERY TOURS, richmondbrewerytours.com

Since 2012, Richmond Brewery Tours has been offering customers an experience to check out the local beer scene in and around Richmond. Tours begin at Capital Ale House, where you get a brief lesson on the basics of beer tasting, then you're off on the bus to travel around to three other breweries. Public tours are offered 3 days every week—Thursday, Friday, and Saturday—and if you so choose, they also offer private tour options.

ROANOKE CRAFT BEER TOURS, roanokefoodtours.com/tours/craft_beer_tour

If you'd like to visit the breweries along the Blue Ridge Beerway but prefer not to do all the driving yourself, then consider the Roanoke Craft Beer Tours. It covers almost all of the breweries along the trail where you can hop on a tour bus (max capacity of 14) for a 4-hour tour, get a minimum of 12 beer tastings, and even a "to go" cheeseburger for the bus.

TASTE TIDEWATER TOURS, tastetidewater.com

For those visiting or living in the coastal Virginia region, Taste Tidewater offers a way to go on a private bus tour that chauffeurs you to multiple breweries through-out the region. There's a Southside Brewery tour that covers Virginia Beach and Norfolk, a Peninsula Breweries tour covering the Williamsburg area stops, or a Virginia Beach Only or Norfolk Only experience. Tours can be customized to meet each group's needs.

Homebrew Shops

ARTISANS WINE & HOMEBREW

13829 Village Place Dr., Midlothian, VA 23114; (804) 379-1110;
artisanswineandhomebrew.com

Building their business "one customer at a time," Cathy and Arthur Allen opened
up for business in October of 2014. They were inspired to get into the business after
Arthur began homebrewing with their son Dave, who started brewing at home on
a Mr. Beer Kit, then eventually advanced to partial mash and to all-grain brewing.
Their inventory includes all the usual ingredients and equipment to make craft beer
and wine, as well as products for making cheese, cider, mead, and soda.

BLUE RIDGE HYDROPONICS & HOME BREWING COMPANY

Williamson Road Plaza, 5327 D Williamson Rd., Roanoke, VA 24012; (540) 265-
2483; blueridgehydroponics.com

Fran and Chris Arthur both worked in the environmental science fields prior to
establishing what started out as a hydroponics gardening business in 2004, then
expanded to include a beer- and wine-making business in 2005. The original concept for the store was established when they "looked for something new to bring
to Southwest Virginia that would be compatible with our work experiences." Since
that original opening, they've relocated twice in order to increase their size—today
they're in a 3,400-square-foot facility. In addition to fulfilling all their customers'
brewing supply needs—novices to highly experienced brewers—they also offer beer-
making and wine-making classes (as well as hydroponics and organic gardening
classes).

HOMEBREW USA

Hampton Location—96 West Mercury Blvd., Hampton, VA 23669; (757) 788-8001
Norfolk Location—5802 E. Virginia Beach Blvd., #115, Norfolk, VA 23502; (757)
459-2739; homebrewusa.com

Originally opened in 2000 in Norfolk, Homebrew USA is a full-service shop. Current
owners Neal and Elizabeth Erschens have done a wonderful job of making it the

place in the region to go each and every time you need to purchase supplies, and Homebrew USA now has two locations in coastal Virginia. Full-service is a great option for many homebrewers, who can bring their recipe in to the store and get the exact ingredients they need down to the ounce. The Homebrew USA store in Norfolk also has a great wall filled with some homebrew recipes to give homebrewers new ideas for their next batch.

JAY'S BREWING SUPPLIES
9790 Center St., Manassas, VA 20110; (703) 543-2663; jaysbrewing.com

This homebrew supply store is in the exact same shopping plaza location as BadWolf Brewing Company. Though the homebrew supply store came way before BadWolf Brewing existed, it's still fortunate that the two places are so close to each other, because after you get excited about all the cool homebrewing-style operation you see going on at BadWolf, and drinking the beer, you can venture over to Jay's Brewing Supplies to get started at home yourself. At the store, "all of the grains, malts, and hops are displayed in self-service containers for you to view, smell, and taste as you wish."

MY LOCAL HOMEBREW SHOP ("MYLHBS")
6201 Leesburg Pike, Falls Church, VA 22044; (703) 241-3874; mylhbs.com

Since the mid '90s, Derek Terrell has been running his own homebrew shop, but his career in the brewing business started much earlier. When he originally started the shop he was both brewing professionally at Potomac River Brewing and running the shop at the same time.

He and the rest of the myLHBS team are all passionate about the brewing industry and it shows when you enter the store as a customer. Derek shared this with me: "When I started myLHBS I was surprised by the number of customers asking for clones of Potomac River Brewing Co. ales so I spent quite some time developing store recipes for just that purpose. Even if you never tried any of our locally produced beer back then, I'm really pleased with how well our kits have been received and I guess this is my way of preserving a bit of local brewing heritage too. In retrospect maybe that's part of what led me to open the shop; business ownership runs in the family and this lets me keep one foot in the brewing world which I know and love." For those who can't get to the store in person, you can also order online via their website.

ORIGINAL GRAVITY
6118 Lakeside Ave., Henrico, VA 23228; (804) 264-4808; oggravity.com

Homebrewing in the Richmond area is a growing hobby, and you can see the proof of its growth when you visit the new Original Gravity homebrew store location. They outgrew the space they started in a few doors away and recently moved to a new space about five times larger. Owner Tony Ammendolia is clearly knowledgeable about the business, having homebrewed for over 20 years himself, and he and his staff are always on hand to answer any of your questions, whether you're a beginner or an advanced homebrewer. In addition to all the products you expect to see at a homebrew store, you should also check out some of the local products they offer, like yeast from RVA Yeast Labs (rvayeastlabs.com). Tony also takes an active role in partnering with other local brewers as well. He recently brewed collaboration beers with his friends and members of the Richmond beer community at breweries like Triple Crossing Brewery and Isley Brewing Company.

One of Tony's other goals was to open up his own brewery one day. That goal is on its way to being met (as soon as he obtains all the necessary licenses). Within the homebrew shop, there is a small bar with 10 tap lines that will supply beer that he makes on a 1-barrel brewing system in the back of the shop, in a soon-to-be new brewery called Final Gravity Brewing. So shop for your homebrew supplies and stay for a beer.

PINTS O' PLENTY
1219 Burnbridge Rd., Forest, VA 24451; (434) 851-5646; pintsoplenty.com

Next door to Apocalypse Ale Works (see Central Virginia chapter), this homebrew store is also run by the same team, Lee and Doug John, who own the firehouse transformed into a brewery next door. After sampling a flight at the brewery, it's an easy walk next door to purchase some brewing supplies for your home if you get inspired to try.

SHENANDOAH VALLEY HOMEBREWING SUPPLIES
17 Middlebrook Ave., Suite 300, Staunton, VA 24401; (540) 887-2337; shenval brew.com

In a historic building in downtown Staunton that was once an old grain mill warehouse, today you can still find certain grains—for your beer supplies. This little store was once a homebrew supply store only, where you could purchase grains, hops, dry extracts, wet extracts, yeast, brewing accessories, brew-kits, kegging equipment, and more. Today, make sure to have enough time to stay for a beer after you buy your supplies. Next to the homebrew store there's now a brewery and tasting room. (See Shenandoah Valley Brewing Company in Shenandoah Valley chapter.)

VALLEY HOMEBREW

199-1 Sulky Dr., Winchester, VA 22602; (540) 868-7616; valleyhomebrew.com

Eric and Kim Boyers noticed something missing in Winchester—the area was severely lacking in homebrew businesses—and being Winchester natives, they set out to fill that gap. So after years of working in the IT field, Eric transitioned from director of technology to homebrew store owner and expert, and he and Kim officially opened up their store for business in April 2012. They hope to spread their passion for homebrewing to others in the Shenandoah Valley and beyond, and part of that mission includes providing "not only quality products and fresh ingredients, but to be a source of knowledge and guidance to new and seasoned hobbyists alike . . . and to bridge the gap between small craft breweries, regional wineries, and the home enthusiast." In addition to beer and wine supplies, it's also set up to help educate others through classes like Beginning Beer Brewing, All-Grain Brewing, and more, and used as a home to the Shenandoah Valley Homebrewers guild.

Clone Beer Recipes

The American Homebrewers Association reports that there are now over 1.2 million people who brew their own beer at home in the US.

Many of the brewers in this book risked it all to start their own breweries, all because of their interest in making good beer and a passion for homebrewing.

Here are some recipes that should help you start (or continue) on your home-brewing journey.

TMAVY DARK CZECH LAGER

Get away from the common styles like IPAs and try out this delicious Czech lager from Lost Rhino Brewing Company. Lost Rhino Brewing's co-founder and brewmaster Favio Garcia says this about the beer: "Mike Stein, historian, homebrewer, and friend of the brewery suggested a few years ago that we should brew a dark Czech lager. Since we at Lost Rhino love our lagers I eagerly agreed. On the first Tmavy brewday Mike and a group of DC homebrewers came by and brewed the batch with us. In the spirit of collaboration and sharing here is my shot at a 5-gallon homebrew recipe for the Dark Czech Lager."

OG 1.057

IBU 35

Expected ABV: 6.2%

Grains:
8 pounds pilsner malt
1 pound 2 ounces Munich
1 pound 2 ounces CaraMunich II

Hops:
.87 ounce Czech Saaz at 90 minutes
.5 ounce Czech Saaz at 60 minutes
1 ounce Czech Saaz at 20 minutes

Yeast:
Lager yeast

Two mash rests at 144° and 154°F. 90-minute boil.

COURTESY OF LOST RHINO BREWING CO. IN ASHBURN, VA (P. 24)

EXPEDITION IPA

Adventure Brewing describes their signature IPA as an "interesting update to plain old IPAs," with the essence of white wine and citrus hops. Homebrewers will be able to share this beer with both IPA lovers and those who are just starting to acquire a taste for IPAs.

OG 1.063

FG 1.019

IBU 35

SRM 13.5

> *Grains:*
> *10.5 pounds 2-row brewers malt*
> *1 pound 2-row caramel malt 60L*
>
> *Hops:*
> *1 ounce Cascade at 60 minutes*
> *1 ounce Falconer's Flight at 15 minutes*
>
> *Yeast:*
> *Safale US-05*

Mash grains at 154°F for 75 minutes.

After 7 days, dry-hop with the following:

1 ounce Citra

1 ounce Nelson Sauvin

COURTESY OF ADVENTURE BREWING IN STAFFORD, VA (P. 4)

ALPHA OX SESSION IPA

Packed with hops and flavor, but lighter in alcohol content than the typical American IPA in today's craft beer marketplace, this homebrew recipe courtesy of Old Ox Brewery is a great one to improve your IPA knowledge and skills.

OG 1.045

FG 1.01

IBU 25

Grains:
6 pounds 1 ounce 2-row pale malt
1 pound 5.2 ounces Munich malt 10L
12.1 ounces Caravienne malt
6.1 ounces Car-Pils/Dextrine
2.5 ounces flaked oats

Hops:
.24 ounce Columbus (Tomahawk) at 15 minutes
.63 ounce Amarillo Gold at 10 minutes
.63 ounce Simcoe at 5 minutes
1.25 ounces Amarillo Gold at 0 minutes
1.25 ounces Columbus at 0 minutes
.62 ounce Centennial at 0 minutes
.62 ounce Simcoe at 0 minutes

Yeast:
.9 pkg American Ale (Wyeast Labs #1056)
.9 pkg Yorkshire Square Ale Yeast (White Labs #WLP037)

Other:
1 tab Whirlfloc at 15 minutes

Add 10.85 quarts of water at 163.7°F (step temperature of 152°F for 60 minutes).

Mash out at 168°F for 10 minutes.

Boil: Add water to achieve boil volume of 6.52 gallons.

Primary fermentation: 4 days at 67°F; Secondary fermentation: 10 days at 67°F.

Dry hop:

.91 ounce Amarillo Gold 3 days

.91 ounce Centennial 3 days

.91 ounce Columbus (Tomahawk) 3 days

Age beer for 30 days at 65°F.

COURTESY OF OLD OX BREWERY IN ASHBURN, VA (P. 34)

GHOST PEPPER GOSE

"Big. Bold. Beer." That's Big Ugly Brewing's motto and this ghost pepper gose recipe proves it, a traditional gose style with the addition of some spicy peppers.

OG: 1.048

FG: 1.012

Estimated ABV: 4.8%

IBU: 13.3

SRM: 3.9

Grains:
3.5 pounds Belgian pilsner
5 pounds German wheat malt
2 pounds acid malt
6 cups unmilled 2-row grain (not to be included with initial mash)

Hops:
0.5 oz Tettnang hops at 60 minutes
0.2 oz Amarillo hops at 60 minutes

Yeast:
Safale US-05

Other:
1 tab Whirlfloc at 10 minutes
0.75 ounce sea salt at 10 minutes
1 ounce ground coriander at 10 minutes
Ghost pepper (your choice as to how much to add/how spicy to make it)

Mash for 60 minutes. Cool wort to 120°F and return wort to empty mash tun. Add 6 cups of unmilled 2-row grain, in a grain bag. Wrap the mash tun in a blanket to keep it warm, and leave in place for at least 8 hours. If you have a ph tester, monitor the ph until it gets below 3.8. If not, taste test until it is moderately sour.

Once desired sourness is achieved, boil for 60 minutes with hop additions and other additions as listed above. Cool, then pitch yeast.

After 1 week, slice a ghost pepper into very thin strips (wear gloves!) and rack beer to secondary, adding tiny amounts of the pepper.

Over the next few days, sample the beer until desired heat is achieved. A little ghost pepper goes a long way, so use sparingly.

COURTESY OF BIG UGLY BREWING IN CHESAPEAKE, VA (P. 150)

In the Kitchen

Beer pairing dinner events at restaurants and breweries across Virginia are now easier to find and attend than ever before. Want to have your own? Consider some of the recipes below as you create a beer and food pairing dinner party for yourself and friends.

WILD WOLF BREWING BEER JELLY

Beer jelly has multiple uses, whether it's adding flavor as a marinade to a home-cooked meal or serving as a dressing or topping for sandwiches, bread, or salads. Wild Wolf Brewing uses it on their mouthwatering Fried Chicken Sandwich, a fried chicken breast from Spruce Creek Farm on Wild Wolf sourdough bread, topped with Swiss and Jalapeno jam made with their own Alpha Ale beer.

YIELD: 1 GALLON

> 72 ounces beer (one sixpack)
> Juice of $1/2$ lemon
> 1 container pectin (4.7 ounces)
> 3 pounds sugar

Add beer to a large pot; slowly bring to a boil.

Boil on medium until foam dissipates back into solution.

Add lemon juice.

Slowly whisk in pectin, dissolve completely.

Add sugar, whisk in while raising heat to a boil, being careful not to burn jelly.

Raise heat slowly, boil for EXACTLY 1 minute while whisking, then remove from heat.

Pour into jars, leave foam on top if you want the final product to resemble "beer."

COURTESY OF MARY AND DANNY WOLF, FOUNDERS OF WILD WOLF BREWING COMPANY IN NELLYSFORD, VA
(P. 104)

WELSH RAREBIT

This is a brown ale horseradish cheese that is served as a small plate at DoG Street Pub over warm toasted bread. DoG Street Pub's American mouthwatering gastropub menu and amazing beer selection is enough to make you stop by, but its location is also ideal in the center of Colonial Williamsburg, where after filling up on some delicious food and drinks, you can stroll around the shops and sites.

YIELD: 12 SERVINGS

    2 tablespoons butter
    3 tablespoons flour
    $^1/_2$ cup ale
    2 cups heavy cream
    2 tablespoons Worcestershire sauce
    1 tablespoon dry mustard
    2 ounces shredded yellow cheddar cheese
    3 ounces Stilton cheese

Make the roux: In a small saucepan, melt the butter over medium heat. Whisk in the flour and cook until the flour is completely incorporated to form a thick, pale roux. Remove from heat and set aside.

In a 2-quart saucepot, bring the ale to a simmer. Whisk in the roux a little at a time until the mixture reaches the consistency of peanut butter; you may not use all of the roux. Whisk in the heavy cream, Worcestershire, and dry mustard. Bring to a simmer again and fold in the cheddar and Stilton cheeses and continue cooking until the mixture is smooth. Remove from heat.

Spread a generous helping of cheese over two slices of thick-cut toasted white bread and melt under a broiler.

COURTESY OF DOG STREET PUB TEAM IN WILLIAMSBURG, VA (P. 166)

STOUT CHILI

Another DoG Street Pub small plate option, this is the perfect tummy-warming snack to go with your craft beer.

YIELD: 1¼ GALLONS OR ABOUT 10 SERVINGS

   5 pounds ground beef
   1 pound diced onions
   3 cups dry or oatmeal stout
   3¼ pounds tomato sauce
   1⅔ pounds red beans
   2¼ teaspoons dark chili powder
   2¼ teaspoons salt
   2¼ teaspoons ancho powder
   2¼ teaspoons ground cumin
   2¼ teaspoons brown sugar
   ¼ cup minced garlic
   ½ cup minced jalapenos
   1½ cup dark chocolate
   Cheddar cheese (as desired)

Saute beef until browned. Strain fat and return to pan. Add onions until tender.

Add next 10 ingredients and simmer for about 45 minutes.

Remove from heat and stir in chocolate until incorporated. Top with cheddar and serve.

COURTESY OF DOG STREET PUB TEAM IN WILLIAMSBURG, VA (P. 166)

CHOCOLATE CARAMEL BREAD PUDDING WITH STOUT CRÈME ANGLAISE

Some stout beers are dessert on their own, but when you combine a rich, full-bodied stout (in this case we suggest the Eye of Jupiter Stout from Belly Love Brewing) with a chocolate caramel bread pudding, you have pure bliss.

YIELD: 10 TO 12 SERVINGS

Chocolate Caramel Bread Pudding

6 croissants, toasted
9 to 10 eggs
1½ quarts cream
2 tablespoons vanilla
¾ cup bourbon
1¼ cups sugar
½ teaspoon salt
1½ cups chocolate chips
1 cup melted caramel

Tear croissants into large pieces, toast in a single layer on a baking sheet until just medium brown in a 350°F oven.

Combine eggs, cream, vanilla, bourbon, sugar, and salt.

Add toasted croissant and let sit for 15 minutes to allow the croissant to soak up some of the egg mixture.

Butter a 9x13x2 baking dish, add croissant mix, and sprinkle with chocolate chips, pushing some down into the pudding and leaving others on the surface.

Pour the caramel in a ribbon over the top of the pudding mixture.

Bake at 350°F for approximately 1 hour, or until center is just set.

Stout Crème Anglaise

YIELD: 2½ QUARTS

1 quart Belly Love Brewing, Eye of Jupiter Oatmeal Stout
1 quart cream
1¾ cups sugar
18 egg yolks
2 teaspoons vanilla extract
Salt to taste

After reducing 1 pint of the stout to 1 cup syrup, recombine with remaining pint of stout.

Add remaining ingredients, mix with an immersion blender till smooth, heat over medium heat, stirring constantly and scraping the bottom of the pan constantly until the custard just coats the back of a wooden spoon.

Remove from heat, pour through a fine mesh strainer and chill, covered, for a few hours. It will thicken a bit as it chills.

RECIPE PROPERTY OF KAREN HARPER-FUOG CATERING IN PURCELLVILLE, VA. SHARED COURTESY OF TOLGA BAKI AT BELLY LOVE BREWING (P. 8)

Appendix A:
Beer Lover's Pick List

Albemarle Amber, C'ville-ian Brewing Co., Amber Ale, 87

Alter Ego Saison, Smartmouth Brewing, Saison, 160

Angry Neighbor Pale Ale, Old 690 Brewing Company, Pale Ale, 30

Angry Scot, Brass Cannon Brewing Company, Scottish Strong Ale, 152

Ape Hanger Russian Imperial Stout, Big Ugly Brewing Company, Imperial Stout, 151

B/A/Y/S (Black As Your Soul) Imperial Stout, Adroit Theory Brewing Company, Imperial Stout, 2

Belgian Blonde, Forge Brew Works, Blonde Ale, 19

Black Dog Stout, Busted Still Brewing, Stout, 171

Black Ox, Old Ox Brewery, Rye Porter, 36

Black Rabbit Stout, Queen City Brewing, Stout, 127

Black Rye IPA, Redbeard Brewing, India Pale Ale, 128

'Choosy Mother' Peanut Butter Oatmeal Porter, Isley Brewing Company, Oatmeal Porter, 63

Dankness Monster, The Damascus Brewery, Imperial Red India Pale Ale, 174

Dark Rye: Black Pepper Series, Ardent Craft Ales, Imperial Stout, 57

El Guapo, O'Connor Brewing Company, India Pale Ale, 154

English IPA, St. George Brewing, India Pale Ale, 161

Eventide IPA, Seven Arrows Brewing Company, India Pale Ale, 132

Expedition IPA, Adventure Brewing, India Pale Ale, 5

Eye of Jupiter, Belly Love Brewing Company, Oatmeal Stout, 9

1st Brigade Red IPA, Shenandoah Valley Brewing, India Pale Ale, 133

Flying Mouse Five, Flying Mouse Brewery, Pale Ale, 124

40-Mile IPA, Three Notch'd Brewing, India Pale Ale, 97

Fred Red Ale, Blue and Gray Brewing Company, Irish Ale, 11

Full Nelson Virginia Pale Ale, Blue Mountain Barrel House/Blue Mountain Brewery, Pale Ale, 81

Get Bent Mountain IPA, Parkway Brewing, India Pale Ale, 125

Gingerbread Stout, Hardywood Park Craft Brewery, Imperial Milk Stout, 60

Graffiti House West Coast IPA, Old Bust Head Brewing Company, India Pale Ale, 34

Grateful Pale Ale, Starr Hill Brewery, Pale Ale, 95

Home Turf, Lost Rhino Brewing Company, Sour/Wild Ale, 25

Hoppocalypse, Apocalypse Ale Works, Imperial Red Ale, 78

Hoptopus, Reaver Beach Brewing Co., Double India Pale Ale, 158

Irish Red Ale, Blue Lab Brewing Company, Irish Ale, 117

Jet Noise, Young Veterans Brewing Company, Double India Pale Ale, 162

La Calvera Cantina, Lickinghole Creek Craft Brewery, Belgian Tripel, 90

Legend Brown Ale, Legend Brewing Company, Brown Ale, 65

Lemon Basil, Backroom Brewery, Wheat Ale, 113

Lesner Sunrise, Pleasure House Brewing, Belgian Single, 155

Little Devil Blonde, Hopkins Ordinary Ale Works, Blonde Ale, 23

Mad Hopper IPA, Chaos Mountain Brewing, India Pale Ale, 120

Missile IPA, Champion Brewing Company, India Pale Ale, 85

My Bitter Valentine, Alewerks Brewing Company, Double India Pale Ale, 147

My Only Friend, Ocelot Brewing Company, Russian Imperial Stout, 27

Nectar & Knife DIPA, Triple Crossing Brewing, Imperial India Pale Ale, 69

"No Veto" English Brown Ale, Three Notch'd Brewing, Harrisonburg, Brown Ale, 139

Oak-Aged Kings Mountain, Heritage Brewing Co., Oak-Aged Scot-American Ale, 21

Oscillate Wildly Blueberry Wild, Strangeways Brewing, Sour Ale, 66

Padawan Pumpkin Ale, Corcoran Brewing Company, Pumpkin Ale, 13

Pocahoptas IPA, Center of the Universe Brewing Company, India Pale Ale, 83

Port City Porter, Port City Brewing Company, Porter, 38

Quayside Kölsch, Fair Winds Brewing Company, Kölsch, 17

Red Clay IPA, Sunken City Brewing Company, India Pale Ale, 175

Resolute Bourbon Barrel Imperial Stout, Brothers Craft Brewing, Imperial Stout, 118

Rockville Red, Midnight Brewery, Irish Red Ale, 92

Roy's Big Bad Brown Ale, Rusty Beavery Brewery, Brown Ale, 93

Rye IPA, Swover Creek Farms—Farm Brewery, India Pale Ale, 137

Shadow of Truth, Crooked Run Brewing, Belgian Dark Ale, 15

Solera Stout, Garden Grove Brewing Company, Stout, 59

Sorachi SMASH, BadWolf Brewing Company, Specialty/Spiced Belgian Ale, 7

Steel Pier Bohemian Lager, Back Bay Brewing Company, Lager, 149

Sterling Stout, Wild Run Brewing Company, Stout, 43

Time the Avenger, Big Lick Brewing Company, India Pale Ale, 115

Track 1, Roanoke Railhouse Brewery, Munich Dunkel Lager, 130

Trailhead Nut Brown Ale, Soaring Ridge Craft Brewers, Nut Brown Ale, 135

Unkel Dunkel, Tin Cannon Brewing, Dunkelweizen, 42

Vienna Lager, Devils Backbone Outpost Brewery, Lager, 123

Wolf Den Double IPA, Wolf Hills Brewing Company, Double India Pale Ale, 178

Appendix B:
Other Newly Opened and
Up & Coming Breweries

What an amazing time for beer in Virginia! Not only are many new brewery projects in the works, with new breweries opening up every day, but this also marks a time when some medium- and large-sized reputable craft brewers, like Stone Brewing and Green Flash Brewing, both based in California, have chosen the state of Virginia—among many other contenders—as their choice for an East Coast hub.

The list below is only a sample list based on recommendations I've received from other brewery owners about up and coming breweries in their regions. To see a much more comprehensive list, you should check out the Virginia Beer Trail website at vabeertrail.net.

Northern Virginia

BARLEY NAKED BREWING
15 Tech Pkwy., Stafford, VA 22554
barleynaked.com
Stafford, Virginia, is on its way to having three breweries in the vicinity: the soon-to-be Barley Naked Brewing, Wild Run Brewing (based at the Aquia Pines Campground resort, just a short 5-mile drive from Barley Naked), and Adventure Brewing, a little farther south.

BARNHOUSE BREWERY
Leesburg, VA
barnhousebrewery.com
Construction is ongoing for this soon-to-be farm brewery and tasting room in the Leesburg area. While that construction is going on, the Barnhouse team is also busy doing some planting—they recently planted 128 hops plants.

CABOOSE BREWERY

520 Mill St. NE, Vienna, VA 22180

caboosebrewing.com

This 15-barrel brewery in the Vienna community of Northern Virginia should be well on its way serving up flights and growlers by the time you read this book. They're expecting to have 8 to 12 beers on tap at all times, and are located at an ideal spot, next to the Washington and Old Dominion Trail, so it will be easy to hike or bike your way to this new brewery.

DIRT FARM BREWING

18701 Foggy Bottom Rd., Bluemont, VA 20135

dirtfarmbrewing.com

The passing of the farm brewery act in 2014 has enabled some exciting new breweries to open up and Dirt Farm Brewing will soon be one of them. It's great when you don't have to go far to get ingredients for your beer—like fruit, hops, and barley that Dirt Farm will both grow and be able to use in their beer recipes.

ORNERY BEER COMPANY

14389 Potomac Mills Rd.

Woodbridge, VA 22192

ornerybeer.com

This future brewpub in Woodbridge, Virginia, looks to be a large and spacious venue with plenty of room for beer geeks everywhere. On their Facebook page, they note that they are "committed to amazing house brewed ales & lagers, complemented by a comforting pub & outstanding chef's menu."

PORTNER BREWHOUSE

Alexandria, VA

portnerbrewhouse.com

Inspired by the Robert Portner Brewing Company, a large pre-Prohibition brewery based in old town Alexandria, this soon to be new brewery will be both a restaurant and a craft beer test kitchen.

SPENCER DEVON BREWING

106 George St.

Fredericksburg, VA 22401

spencerdevonbrewing.com

Co-founder Shawn Phillips and his wife, Lisa, have recently opened Spencer Devon Brewing, now the second brewery in the city of Fredericksburg along with Blue

& Gray Brewing. Their philosophy is to bring the "highest quality craft beer dining experience to the Fredericksburg region." To do that, they've hired chef Justin Cunningham and head brewer John Ritenour, who both have years of experience in their industries and are passionate about serving up some memorable food and beer to the Fredericksburg community.

TWINPANZEE BREWING CO.
1390 Chain Bridge Rd., #2008, McLean, VA 22101
twinpanzee.com

Many brewers these days are emphasizing keeping it local and forging ties with the community. Twinpanzee seems to be one of them, as they announce on their Facebook page that they are the "first craft brewery in Fairfax County started by primates born & raised in Fairfax County."

Central Virginia

FINAL GRAVITY
6118 Lakeside Ave., Henrico, VA 23228

First a homebrew shop, soon to be a homebrew shop and taproom, owner Tony Ammendolia is in the process of securing the permits to introduce customers to some of his new beer concoctions from a 1-barrel brew system that can be seen from the back of the homebrew store through glass windows.

JAMES RIVER BREWERY
561 Valley St., Scottsville, VA 24590
jamesriverbrewing.com

The 19th-century tobacco warehouse that James River Brewery is based in was previously used as a brewery beginning in 2012, but the first two business attempts were unsuccessful. It's now back as of 2015 with a new owner and management team, and there's a beer garden along a creek, a taproom, and live music on most weekends. Nearby restaurants deliver food to the brewery.

LOOSE SHOE BREWING
198 Ambriar Plaza, Amherst, VA 24521
looseshoebrewing.com

Owners Derin and Kitty Foor have created a new brewery for the Amherst County community and are making that beer on a 1-barrel brew system. Derin's background as a farrier (horseshoer) is evident when you visit the tasting room. Try beers like the Vixenbier, a Vienna lager, and the Blacksmith, an imperial Irish stout. Their taproom is now open Thursday through Sunday.

7 HILLS BREWING COMPANY
115 S. 15th St., Richmond, VA 23219

Soon to be coming to Shockoe Bottom in Richmond, this brewery/brewpub will be situated in a prime location and will be within walking distance for those staying in the downtown area, making it an easy place to add to your next craft beer pub crawl.

STEAM BELL BREW WORKS
Midlothian, VA

Founder Brad Cooper was born and raised in this area of Virginia. He saw the emergence of all the breweries in Richmond and recognized that residents of his town loved the breweries but also didn't always want to drive into the city of Richmond to get to one. Fortunately Midlothian will soon have its own local spot. Brad invested in a 7-barrel system and is focusing on creating a wide variety of sour and funky beers, as well as using alternative fermentation methods for Steam Bell Brew Works.

STONE BREWING
Williamsburg Avenue & Nicholson Street, Richmond, VA 23231
stonebrewing.com

There's lots of excitement about the new Stone Brewing facility in Richmond. Plans are for a 200,000-square-foot production brewery, packaging hall, destination restaurant, and administrative offices for its East Coast facility in the Great Fulton community of Richmond.

VICTORY BREWPUB
Courthouse Square, East Market Street, Leesburg, VA 20175
victorybeer.com

Victory Brewpub is going all out for its first brewpub outside of its home state of Pennsylvania with this new location in historic Leesburg. According to Victory's website, "Victory at Courthouse Square, the fourth Victory brewpub, will feature a 300-seat restaurant, upper-level terraces for outdoor dining, and an extensive chef-inspired menu highlighting many of the company's signature dishes."

Shenandoah Valley

PALE FIRE BREWING
217 South Liberty St. #105, Harrisonburg, VA 22801
palefirebrewing.com
A new brewery in downtown Harrisonburg is now upping Harrisonburg's craft beer status, along with breweries like Three Notch'd Brewing, Brothers Craft Brewing, and beer bars like Jack Brown's Beer and Burger Joint and Capital Ale House.

Coastal Virginia

BENCH TOP BREWING
Suffolk, VA
Pilot batches are being brewed for a new planned brewery in Suffolk. Look out for their beer at some upcoming events in the Hampton Roads area.

BOLD MARINER BREWING COMPANY
Norfolk, VA
boldmariner.com
Currently in construction stages, this brewery founded by Michael Stacks is the soon-to-be newest addition to Norfolk's craft beer scene.

COELACANTH BREWING
Norfolk, VA
coelacanthbrewing.com
Named after a giant, bottom-dwelling fish, the Coelacanth Brewing team includes Kevin Erskine and Matt Topping, who are in the planning and construction stages for their brewery in the Norfolk region.

GREEN FLASH BREWERY
1902 General Booth Blvd., Virginia Beach, VA 23228
greenflashbrew.com
With a 100,000-barrel brewing facility all housed in a 58,000-square-foot building, and only a 15-minute drive from the beach, this second Green Flash Brewery (that closely replicates their original San Diego brewery) should be a site to see, with an expected opening of 2016.

RIP RAP BREWING COMPANY

116 East 25th St., Norfolk, VA 23517

riprapbrewing.com

After having met at the Coast Guard Academy, owners Liam Bell and Ben Mcelroy moved onto homebrewing together, and soon decided their next focus should be taking their love of homebrewing and turning it into a business.

THE VIRGINIA BEER COMPANY

401 2nd St., Williamsburg, VA 23185

virginiabeerco.com

With a slogan of "For Our Common Wealth" and the name Virginia Beer Company, all Virginia residents will probably want to make a point to get to Williamsburg to check this place out and see all that's in store for its future plans.

WASSERHUND BREWING COMPANY

1805 Laskin Rd., Suite 102, Virginia Beach, VA 23454

wasserhundbrewing.com

Wasserhund is focusing on brewing German-style beers, and on their website, they share that Wasserhund—"meaning *water dog* in German, was born from a love of the beach, dogs, and German beer."

Southwest Virginia

BRISTOL BREWERY

41 Piedmont Ave., Bristol, VA

bristolbrew.com

Not far from the border separating Virginia from Tennessee, Bristol Brewery boasts a 10-barrel system in a historic bus station in downtown Bristol.

Index